PERFECT DAY CHICAGO

Grab-and-Go Itineraries for Everyone

Wendy Altschuler

Reedy Press
PO Box 5131
St. Louis, MO 63139
www.reedypress.com

Library of Congress Control Number: 2022949035

ISBN: 9781681064352

All photos are by the author unless otherwise noted.

Title page images *(clockwise from top left)*:
1-6. Courtesy of Christine Pejoski @tinetinetinep
7. Courtesy of Wendy Altschuler
8. Courtesy of Ranvestel Photographic, Choose Chicago

Printed in the United States of America
23 24 25 26 27   5 4 3 2 1

Dedication

To my wild and beautiful sons, Bridger, Sage, and Kai;
and to my husband, Scott, without whom this book
would have been completed much sooner.
Dear boys, work hard, be kind,
and amazing things will happen—I promise.

Courtesy of Wendy Altschuler

PERFECT DAY CHICAGO

Grab-and-Go Itineraries for Everyone

REEDY PRESS

Courtesy cf Wendy Altschuler

Contents

Insets above (left to right):
Courtesy of Wendy Altschuler, Courtesy of Wendy Altschuler, Courtesy of Ranvestel Photographic, Choose Chicago, Courtesy of Wendy Altschuler, Courtesy of Wendy Altschuler, Courtesy of Wendy Altschuler

Courtesy of Christine Pejoski @tinetinetinep

Introduction

Time and development have shifted Chicago's boundaries, yet the city is still divided into 77 community areas that are distinct from, but related to, more than 200 diverse neighborhoods. Further geographic splits are created by the Chicago River—"sides," proudly represented by the white stripes on Chicago's flag.

Even with its gleaming glass and steel skyline, the Windy City has always been known as a city of neighborhoods, and whether you're a dyed-in-the-wool local or an out-of-towner, you'll discover something new here. With this guidebook full of itineraries, you can spend the day exploring the lakefront, wandering through the first planetarium in the Western Hemisphere, cheering in the second-oldest ballpark, dancing at one of the more than 70 music festivals, or seeing a performance in a live theater venue. While popular attractions like the Art Institute of Chicago, Navy Pier, Millennium Park, and Willis Tower are included here, lesser-known neighborhood gems are as well.

As someone who has spent over half her life in Chicagoland, first as a college student and later as a mother, roller derby player, and professional travel writer, I can tell you that this global city, sprinkled with Midwestern charm, is unlike any other.

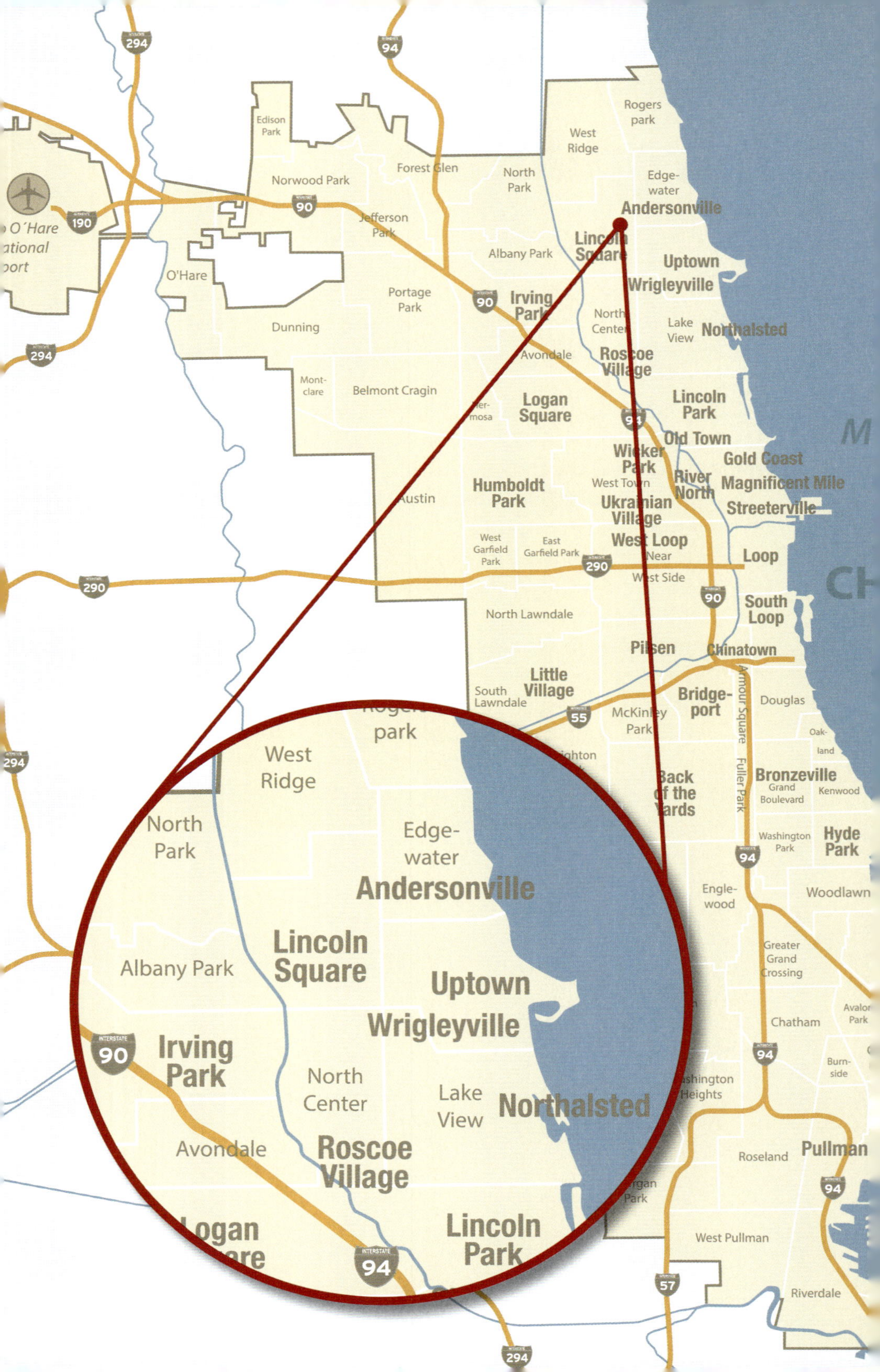

Edison Park
Norwood Park
Forest Glen
North Park
West Ridge
Rogers park
Edge-water
Andersonville
Jefferson Park
Albany Park
Lincoln Square
Uptown
Wrigleyville
O'Hare
O'Hare International Airport
Portage Park
Irving Park
North Center
Lake View
Northalsted
Dunning
Avondale
Roscoe Village
Mont-clare
Belmont Cragin
Logan Square
Lincoln Park
Old Town
Wicker Park
Gold Coast
Humboldt Park
West Town
River North
Magnificent Mile
Austin
Ukrainian Village
Streeterville
West Garfield Park
East Garfield Park
West Loop
Near West Side
Loop
South Loop
North Lawndale
Pilsen
Chinatown
Little Village
South Lawndale
Bridge-port
McKinley Park
Douglas
Armour Square
Fuller Park
Oak-land
Back of the Yards
Bronzeville
Grand Boulevard
Kenwood
Washington Park
Hyde Park
Engle-wood
Woodlawn
Greater Grand Crossing
Chatham
Avalon Park
Burn-side
Washington Heights
Roseland
Pullman
West Pullman
Riverdale
Morgan Park

ANDERSONVILLE

KNOWN AS THE "shop local capital of Chicago," Andersonville, located in Edgewater on Chicago's North Side, is full of independently owned boutiques and eateries, including candy stores, toy shops, and ice cream parlors. Stroll down the Clark Street strip, where an iconic water tower emblazoned with the Swedish flag beckons overhead, and you'll find a slew of Swedish bakeries, a heritage museum with family-friendly programing, and weekly story times in a long-standing bookstore. Venture off Clark and you'll unearth quirky live theater, 19th-century row houses, and distinctive antique shops. Travel east and you'll hit Chicago's Lakefront Trail, Edgewater Dog Park, and Foster Beach.

Home to one of Chicago's largest LGBTQ+ communities, Andersonville is a diverse, supportive, and inclusive community full of exciting events and festivals, where you'll see young parents pushing strollers down the street past historic architecture, couples holding hands while sipping espresso in a corner coffee shop, and friends chatting over brunch at a sidewalk café. Relatively petite and densely packed, this neighborhood is easy to explore on foot with kids in tow.

Women & Children First

25233 N. Clark St. • 773-769-9299 • www.womenandchildrenfirst.com

✔ In business since 1979, **Women & Children First** is everything you want an independent bookstore to be. The staff is warm and welcoming to all, and book recommendations are their forte—no matter what you're looking for, someone here can point you in the right direction.

The store fosters a strong and well-read community and hosts multiple book clubs, author events, and insightful programs for kids and families, whether you're just visiting or are a denizen of Chicago. **The Kids First Book Group**, which includes special activities and crafts, is perfect for kids between the ages of eight and 12. Young children aged two to five can join the weekly story time, which is a fun way to discover new books, socialize with others, and get a slice of that good old neighborhood feel that Andersonville is well known for.

Women & Children First (Courtesy of Women & Children First)

Swedish American Museum (Courtesy of Swedish American Museum)

Swedish American Museum

5211 N. Clark St. • 773-728-8111 • www.swedishamericanmuseum.org

✔ Andersonville's Swedish roots date back to the 19th century, and the **Swedish American Museum** has been educating visitors on the history and culture of Chicago's "Little Sweden" for over 40 years. This 24,000-square-foot museum, which includes the **Brunk Children's Museum of Immigration**, is an important slice of the community with its gallery spaces, art displays, and museum store. The main exhibit, The Dream of America: Swedish Immigration to Chicago, delves into the saga, challenges, and achievements of the Swedish people as they made their way to the Windy City in search of a better life.

Swedish customs and traditions are celebrated, honored, and preserved through instructive, family-friendly programs and events that keep the wider community engaged. Whether you want to practice Scandinavian dance; learn the Swedish language; or take part in festivals like **Midsommarfest**, an annual summer street jubilee, full of music, dancing, food and entertainment; the museum is a boundless resource.

Replay Andersonville

5358 N. Clark St. • 773-654-1369 • www.replayandersonville.com

✔ Dozens of vintage video arcade games and pinball machines are the major draw of **Replay Andersonville**, a casual refuge for not only human-powered entertainment, but also casual house-made dishes with locally sourced ingredients. Watch the big game with your family or friends. For weekend brunch, order the green eggs and ham or find something off the designated kids' menu. Families with children under 18 will have the best time during the week between noon and 6:30 p.m. and on weekends between 10:00 a.m. and 2:00 p.m.

Show your kids how games used to be played, when *Donkey Kong* and *Ms. Pac-Man* reigned supreme, well before everything morphed into online gaming with wireless controllers and headgear. Lively and well located, Replay is a fun spot for adults too, as there are plenty of local craft beers to sample. Traveling with a pet in tow? Dogs are welcome on the alfresco terrace.

Replay Andersonville
(Courtesy of Replay Andersonville)

Nearby Alternatives

Shop: The Wooden Spoon

Family owned, the Wooden Spoon, a staple in the community, is a mecca for innovative kitchen products and insightful cooking classes. Pick out bakeware, gadgets, or cookbooks. Learn how to make a dish in the demonstration kitchen. An outdoor patio with a pizza oven and garden creates an oasis in the city.

5047 N. Clark St.
773-293-3190
www.woodenspoonchicago.com

Shop: On the Rocks

This locally owned small Andersonville business is a top place to go for minerals, fossils, handmade jewelry, and raw and tumbled rocks from all over the world. Let your kid pick out a shiny pocket souvenir or purchase a meaningful gift for a loved one.

5709 N. Clark St.
773-649-0111
www.ontherockschicago.com

Eat: First Slice Pie Café

After exploring the neighborhood on foot, you'll likely need to take a small break. You'll want to stick a fork in a fruit or cream pie—served by the slice or in a mini pie form—or a cheesecake while at First Slice Pie Café, a neighborhood favorite.

5357 N. Ashland Ave.
773-275-4297
www.firstslice.org

Shop: AlleyCat Comics

Part of the fun of AlleyCat Comics is finding it. A sign featuring a black cat hangs over a gate, luring the curious down a pathway to a true lair, a repository of stories from multiple universes where there is something for all. The children's section contains graphic novels and board games.

5304 N. Clark St., Rear Ste.
773-907-3404
www.alleycatcomics.com

Trip Planning

Andersonville Chamber of Commerce

5217 N. Clark St., #3
773-728-2995
www.andersonville.org

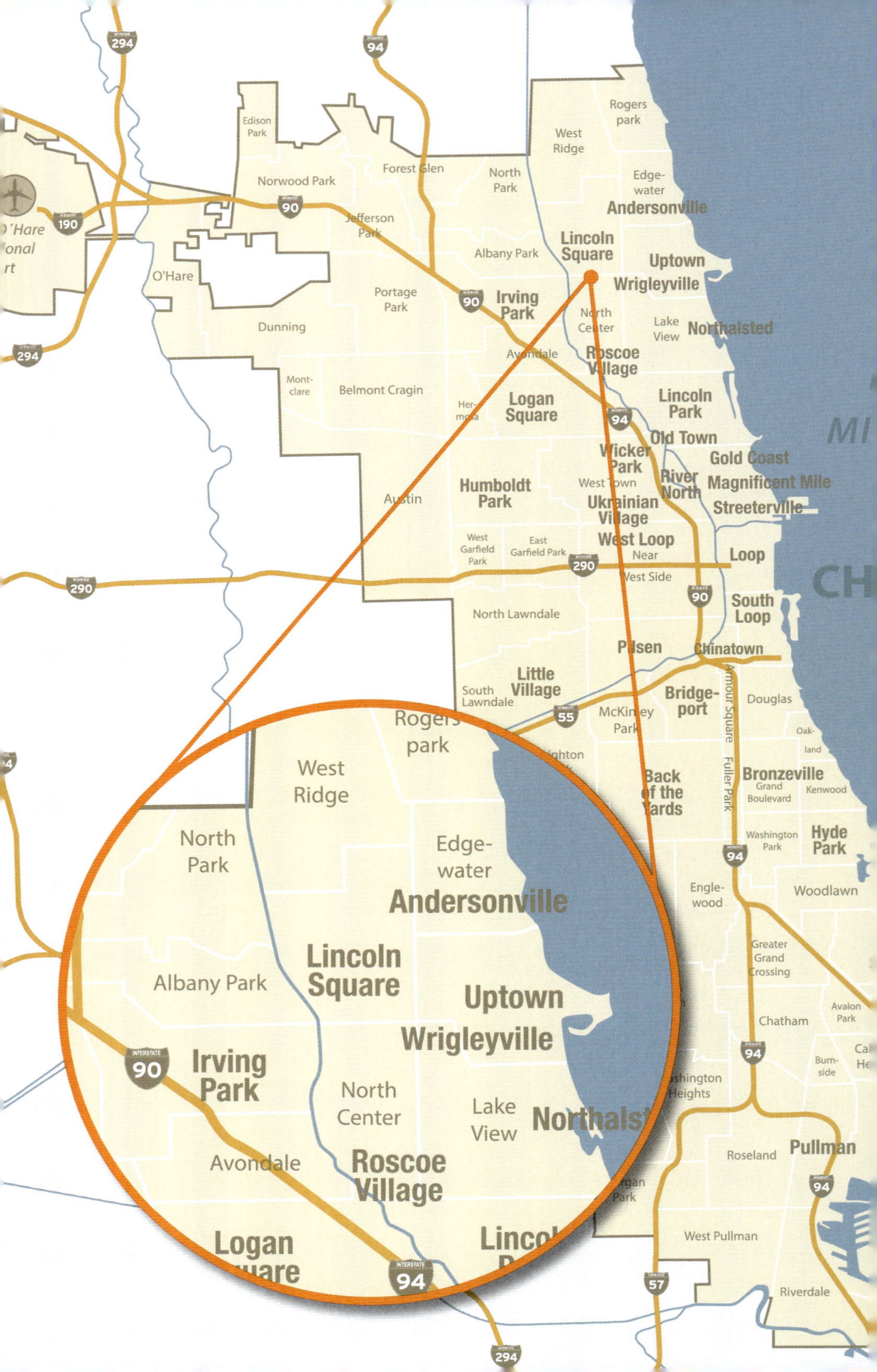

Rogers park
West Ridge
Edgewater
Andersonville
North Park
Edison Park
Norwood Park
Forest Glen
Jefferson Park
Albany Park
Lincoln Square
Uptown
Wrigleyville
O'Hare
Portage Park
Irving Park
North Center
Lake View
Northalsted
Dunning
Avondale
Roscoe Village
Montclare
Belmont Cragin
Hermosa
Logan Square
Lincoln Park
Old Town
Wicker Park
Gold Coast
Austin
Humboldt Park
West Town
River North
Magnificent Mile
Ukrainian Village
Streeterville
West Garfield Park
East Garfield Park
West Loop
Near West Side
Loop
South Loop
North Lawndale
Pilsen
Chinatown
South Lawndale
Little Village
McKinley Park
Bridgeport
Armour Square
Douglas
Oakland
Back of the Yards
Fuller Park
Bronzeville
Grand Boulevard
Kenwood
Washington Park
Hyde Park
Englewood
Woodlawn
Greater Grand Crossing
Avalon Park
Chatham
Burnside
Washington Heights
Roseland
Pullman
Morgan Park
West Pullman
Riverdale
294
94
90
190
290
55
57

LINCOLN SQUARE

FOUNDED BY GERMAN immigrants on the North Side, Lincoln Square is home to Ravenswood, Ravenswood Gardens, Bowmanville, Budlong Woods, and the eponymous Lincoln Square.

Known for microbreweries on "malt row" (Begyle Brewing Company, Dovetail Brewery, Empirical Brewery), DANK Haus German American Cultural Center, boutique shopping, parks, and public art (Berlin Wall Monument in the Western Ave. Brown Line station, Chicago Lincoln Statue at the intersection of Western, Lawrence, and Lincoln), this locale has much to explore. With European-style cafés, Bavarian bakeries, and events like Restaurant Week, German American Oktoberfest, Apple Fest, Square Roots, and Maifest, you'll find plenty to do, especially around the cultural hub, Giddings Plaza, where the annual Summer Concert Series is held. History buffs will value Rosehill Cemetery, Chicago's oldest and largest cemetery, where notable citizens of Chicago rest. Grab a Chicago-style hot dog at Budacki's Drive In; snap a photo in front of the landmark Merz Apothecary, established in 1875; pop into Amy's Candy Bar; shop at Enjoy, An Urban General Store; treat the kids at Timeless Toys; and pursue nostalgic favorites at Quake Collectibles.

Old Town School of Folk Music

4544 N. Lincoln Ave.
773-728-6000
www.oldtownschool.org

✔ North of Welles Park, Old Town School of Folk Music, founded in 1957, is a haven for dance, theater, music, and visual arts. The largest nonprofit community arts school in the US, it offers experiences for all. One-time workshops are a great way to get a taste of internationally inspired classes that focus on singing, Chinese or Bollywood dance, ukulele or banjo fundamentals, or a myriad of other options.

Old Town is known for hosting kids' concerts and family events, global dance parties, and a weekly showcase of world music and dance. Peek in the **Old Town School Music Store** for instruments, resources, and accessories. Check out the Second Half daily jam—free and open to all—or, if you have a talented youth, try the **Teen Open Mic**. Other locations are found in Lincoln Park and the South Loop, with Wiggleworms kids' programs open in branches throughout Chicagoland.

Old Town School of Folk Music
(Courtesy of Adam Alexander Photography, Choose Chicago)

Lillstreet Art Center
(Courtesy of Powell Photography, Choose Chicago)

Lillstreet Art Center

4401 N. Ravenswood Ave. • 773-769-4226 • www.lillstreet.com

A stalwart community of artists and students, **Lillstreet Art Center**, part of the **Ravenswood ArtWalk**, offers a plethora of imaginative meetups for all ages, everything from ceramics to drawing, bookbinding, painting, metalsmithing, printmaking, and photography. The center is open to the public, and folks can join themed one-day workshops to learn and create something fun together. See innovative exhibitions in the gallery space and take a treasure home from the shop.

Multigenerational families or groups of friends will enjoy a private Chicago art party. For up to three hours, a professional teaching artist will lead an immersive experience in a reserved studio, customizing the class to your event's needs and interests. Popular activities include jewelry making, screen printing, ceramics, and painting—aprons and basic art supplies are included. The best part: everyone will leave with a handmade souvenir and memories of time well spent.

Bistro Campagne

4518 N. Lincoln Ave. • 773-271-6100 • www.bistrocampagne.com

✔ It's difficult to choose just one eatery to visit given the breadth of diverse restaurants in this neighborhood. **Gather**, **Cobblestone**, **the Warbler**, **Lutz**, **Café Selmarie**, **Gideon Welles**, and **Rockwell's Neighborhood Grill** are all local favorites. A standout, however, is **Bistro Campagne**, a verdant oasis in the city and a paragon of French cuisine. You'll find that you linger a bit longer as you savor the delectable dishes in the outdoor garden until your belly is full. The 1920s Arts and Crafts–style building, with lovely woodwork throughout, creates a cozy and rustic ambience. Parents who favor French dining yet worry about bringing their brood out to eat can breathe a sigh of relief because not only is the cuisine organic and sustainably sourced, but the walled-in courtyard with ambient lighting creates a relaxing and unpretentious environment for families. Be sure to make a reservation to secure a coveted table.

Bistro Campagne (Courtesy of Wendy Altschuler)

Nearby Alternatives

Discover: Davis Theater

Originally known as the Pershing Theater, the Davis Theater has been part of the community since 1918, when it showcased vaudeville and silent films. Puppet shows, films, and other entertainment were presented through the 1970s. Now this historic landmark is a haven for moviegoers and popcorn crunchers.

4614 N. Lincoln Ave.
773-769-3999
www.davistheater.com

Play: Bloom Yoga Studio

Specializing in prenatal, restorative, and children's yoga, Bloom Yoga Studio is a welcoming space for all ages and levels of fitness. This independent small business, which also has a shop with books, music, clothing, and yoga necessities, has been a home-grown pick since 2004. Massages are also available for holistic care.

4663 N. Rockwell St.
773-463-9642
www.bloomyogastudio.com

Eat: Gene's Sausage Shop and Delicatessen

From Roscoe St. to Belmont Ave., two immigrant brothers from Poland ran a smoked sausage shop. In 2009, a second European market opened in Lincoln Square in the same spot that was once the Delicatessen Meyer, a German American business that lasted 53 years. Enjoy handmade sausage, made daily, on the rooftop garden.

4750 N. Lincoln Ave.
773-728-7243
www.genessausage.com

Shop: The Book Cellar

Not every bookstore allows patrons to sip wine while perusing titles (the café offers a selection of wine, beer, sandwiches, and pastries). From author events, book clubs, reading challenges, and programs for families, the Book Cellar goes above and beyond in its commitment to the community.

4736 N. Lincoln Ave.
773-293-2665
www.bookcellarinc.com

Trip Planning

Lincoln Square Ravenswood Chamber of Commerce

2611 W. Lawrence Ave.
Ground Floor
773-728-3890

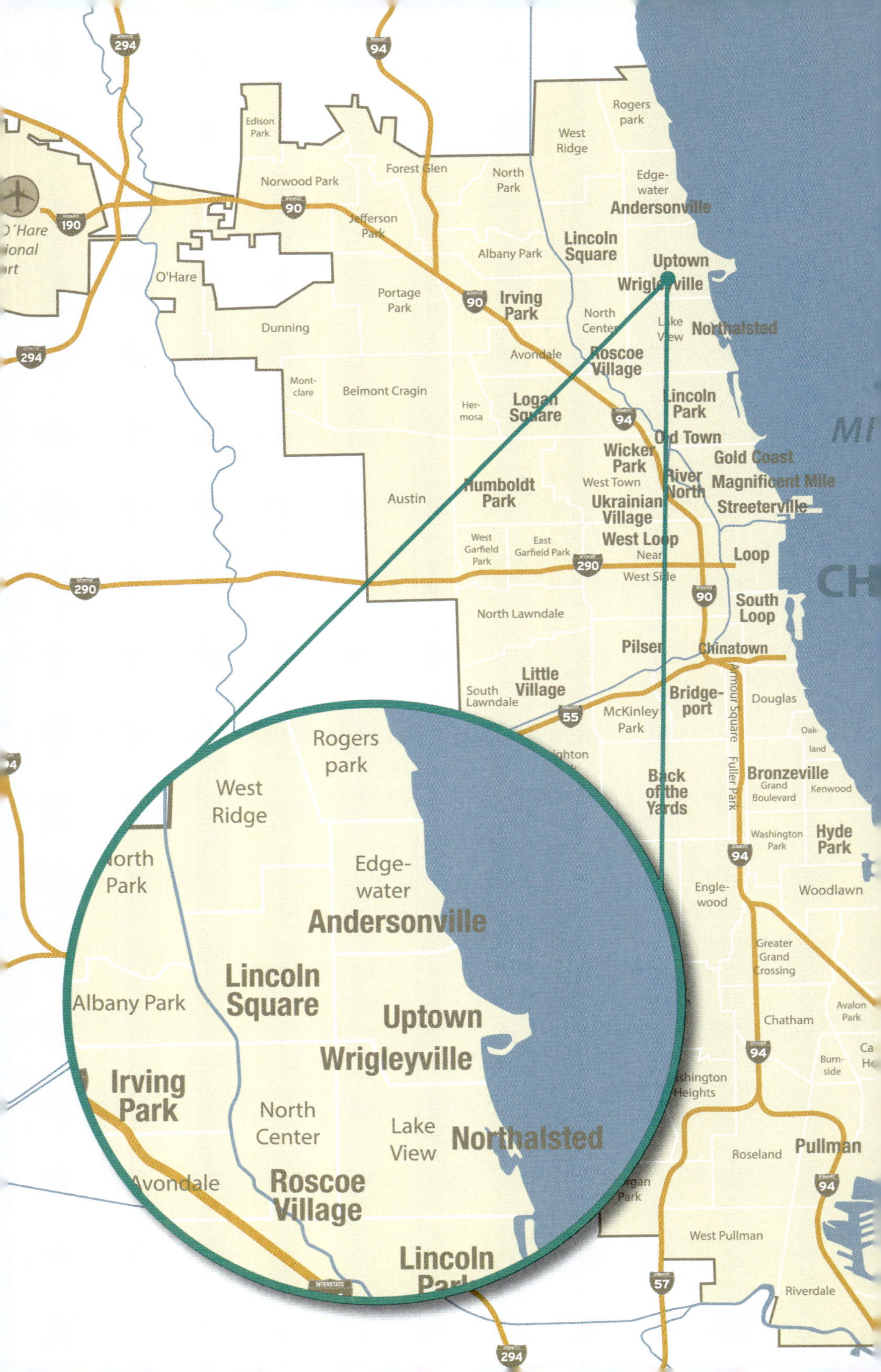
Edison Park
Norwood Park
Forest Glen
North Park
West Ridge
Rogers park
Edge-water
Andersonville
Jefferson Park
Albany Park
Lincoln Square
Uptown
Wrigleyville
O'Hare
Portage Park
Irving Park
North Center
Lake View
Northalsted
Dunning
Avondale
Roscoe Village
Mont-clare
Belmont Cragin
Her-mosa
Logan Square
Lincoln Park
Old Town
Wicker Park
Gold Coast
West Town
River North
Magnificent Mile
Austin
Humboldt Park
Ukrainian Village
Streeterville
West Garfield Park
East Garfield Park
West Loop
Near West Side
Loop
South Loop
North Lawndale
Pilsen
Chinatown
South Lawndale
Little Village
McKinley Park
Bridge-port
Armour Square
Douglas
Oak-land
Back of the Yards
Fuller Park
Bronzeville
Grand Boulevard
Kenwood
Washington Park
Hyde Park
Engle-wood
Woodlawn
Greater Grand Crossing
Avalon Park
Chatham
Burn-side
Roseland
Pullman
West Pullman
Riverdale
MI
CH
294
94
190
90
290
55
57

UPTOWN

EXPLORE ONE OF Chicago's most dynamic neighborhoods with an extensive entertainment history. Uptown's influence spans the Gilded Age, the silent film era, the big band, jazz, and swing ages, and the rock 'n' roll movement. The Aragon Ballroom (1926), Riviera Theater (1917), Uptown Theater (1925), and Green Mill (1907) are all situated near the intersection of Lawrence and Broadway. Graceland Cemetery, listed on the National Register of Historic Places, is where you'll find the final resting places of Ernie Banks, Marshal Field, Roger Ebert, Potter Palmer, and George Pullman.

Within Uptown, you'll discover the fast-changing neighborhoods of Buena Park, known for prairie-style architecture; Sheridan Park, a mostly residential area with a historic district; Argyle Street, also known as "Asia on Argyle," "Little Saigon," and "Little Vietnam"; and Margate Park, full of historic buildings from the 1890s to the 1920s. Many sites in this area are linked to infamous gangsters—John Dillinger, Al Capone, Jack McGurn, and Roger Touhy. A microcosm of Chicago with its lakefront, global cuisine, and diverse population, Uptown has long been a refuge for performers, artists, entrepreneurs, and immigrants.

Montrose Point Bird Sanctuary

200 W. Montrose Harbor Dr. • 312-742-7529
www.chicagoparkdistrict.com

Along Lake Michigan, you'll discover **Montrose Dog Beach**; **Montrose Beach**, ideal for families who want to swim, picnic, kayak, and enjoy skyline views; **Montrose Beach Dunes Natural Area**, vital for shore birds and the endangered Great Lakes piping plover; **Montrose Moonrise Observation Point One**, found on a trail that rounds the harbor; and **Montrose Point Bird Sanctuary**, a prairie, savanna, and woodland natural area that supports thousands of migratory birds. See "The Magic Hedge," a shrub- and tree-filled space where you can hear a symphony of warblers, thrushes, purple martins, woodpeckers, and owls.

This protected area is largely maintained by volunteers. The Chicago Park District runs a Community Stewardship Program, which is a great way not only to learn about native Illinois plants and wildlife, but also to take part in conservation restoration. The **Honeycomb Project** is another nonprofit aggregator that connects families with eco-friendly volunteer projects around the city.

Montrose Beach, Dog Beach
(Courtesy of Wendy Altschuler)

Graceland Cemetery (Courtesy of mikeriveraphoto.com, Graceland Cemetery)

Graceland Cemetery and Arboretum

4001 N. Clark St. • 773-525-1105 • www.gracelandcemetery.org

A hidden gem, **Graceland Cemetery**, established in 1860, offers something for history and architecture buffs and lovers of green spaces alike. Wander 119 acres and see not only the resting places of prominent Chicagoans—entrepreneurs, athletes, architects, and politicians (14 Chicago mayors are buried here)—but also three historic buildings situated on the Victorian park–style grounds. Certified as an arboretum by **Chicago's Morton Arboretum** (also worth a visit), Graceland Cemetery is home to over 2,000 trees.

See pioneering landscape design via the **Tree Tour**, where you can take your family on a nature walk. The southeast corner is home to a restored prairie, a shutterbug's dream. A self-guided audio tour informs listeners about 30 special sites, including monuments and tombs that were designed by architectural virtuosos. Later, when you stroll the city's streets, go past illustrious buildings, or cheer at a baseball game, you'll feel more connected knowing a piece of Chicago's history.

Everybody's Coffee

935 W. Wilson Ave. • 773-303-6220 • www.everybodyscoffee.com

There's a certain community vibe at this café, once a skateboard shop, that you can't find anywhere else in the city. Reflecting the multiplicity of cultures in Chicago, the ethos here is that everyone deserves great coffee. Partnering with **Cornerstone Community Outreach**, a nonprofit that helps Chicago families experiencing homelessness, this Uptown coffee house does more than sling fair-trade Joe.

Creative types who want a millennial-friendly ambience, as well as young parents with kids in tow, can order a cold brew, espresso, or pour-over at the bar fashioned out of reclaimed stone. Expect multi-hued food options like avocado toast with watermelon radishes, house-made pastries and baked goods, bacon and cheddar bagels, sandwiches, and toothsome veggie bowls with seasonal ingredients. For littles, order off the kids' menu. The energy here, where artists, writers, families, and retired neighbors connect and converse, is palpable. Venture out and spot the **Everybody's Coffee** bicycle, pouring nitro coffee on-the-go.

Everybody's Coffee
(Courtesy of Wendy Altschuler)

Nearby Alternatives

Discover: Clifton Avenue Street Art Gallery

Near the Wilson train station, the vibrant Clifton Avenue Street Art Gallery, supported by multiple community initiatives, is where you can spot over 70 large-scale outdoor murals, created from artists around the world. You'll be inspired on this art walk without spending a penny.

Clifton Ave., between Leland Ave. and Wilson Ave.
773-878-1064
www.exploreuptown.org

Discover: Green Mill Jazz Club

A favorite of mobster Al Capone during the Prohibition era, Green Mill is a quintessential must-see spot. *Ocean's 12*, *High Fidelity*, and *Prelude to a Kiss* were filmed here. With nightly live music and the Uptown Poetry Slam Sundays, the Green Mill is a Chicago music and entertainment hub.

4802 N. Broadway Ave.
773-878-5552
www.greenmilljazz.com

Discover: Asia on Argyle

Best explored on foot, **Chicago's West Argyle Street Historic District** is a prime example of how a neighborhood can fuse together rich cultural enclaves with urban renewal. Surrounding the "L" station, an area with pulsating street art and a plethora of Vietnamese and Southeast Asian fare, the **Argyle Night Markets** aren't to be missed.

Argyle St., between Broadway St. and Sheridan Rd.
www.celebrateargylechicago.com

Discover: Black Ensemble Theater

What started as a small community arts organization has blossomed into an internationally known, diverse arts institution with a 170-seat theater. With original plays and musicals that highlight Black stories, as well as community outreach programs that get youth engaged in theater arts, the Black Ensemble Theater is a local gem.

4450 N. Clark Ave.
773-769-4451
www.blackensembletheater.org

Trip Planning

Uptown Chamber of Commerce
4619 N. Broadway Ave.
773-878-1064
www.exploreuptown.org

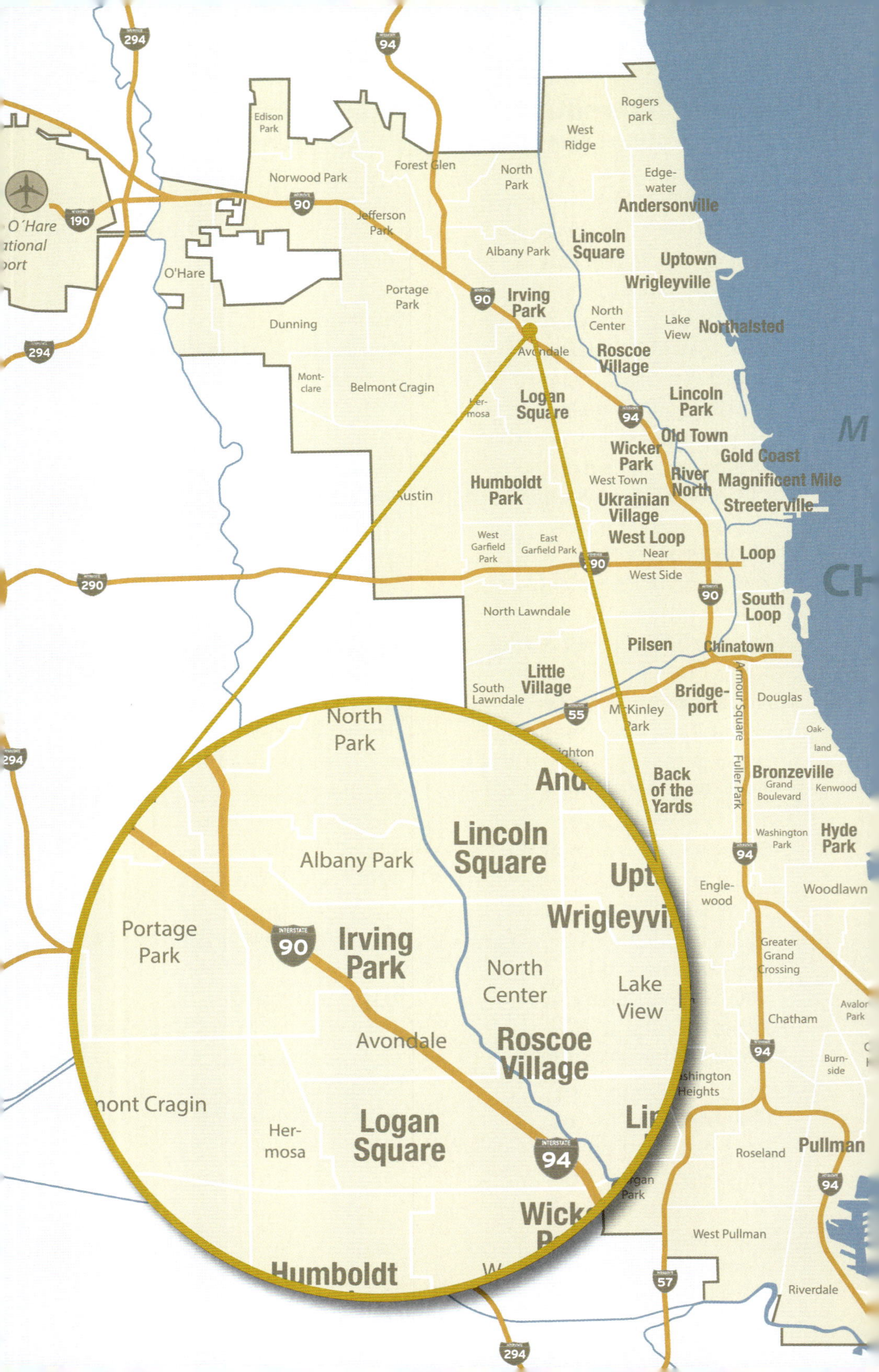

294
94
Edison Park
Rogers park
West Ridge
Norwood Park
Forest Glen
North Park
Edge-water
Andersonville
190
90
Jefferson Park
Albany Park
Lincoln Square
Uptown
O'Hare
Wrigleyville
Portage Park
90
Irving Park
North Center
Lake View
Northalsted
Dunning
294
Avondale
Roscoe Village
Mont-clare
Belmont Cragin
Her-mosa
Logan Square
Lincoln Park
94
Old Town
Wicker Park
Gold Coast
Humboldt Park
West Town
River North
Magnificent Mile
Austin
Ukrainian Village
Streeterville
West Garfield Park
East Garfield Park
West Loop
Near West Side
Loop
290
290
90
South Loop
North Lawndale
Pilsen
Chinatown
Little Village
South Lawndale
55
McKinley Park
Bridge-port
Armour Square
Douglas
Oak-land
294
Fuller Park
Back of the Yards
Bronzeville
Grand Boulevard
Kenwood
Washington Park
Hyde Park
94
Engle-wood
Woodlawn
Greater Grand Crossing
Chatham
Avalon Park
94
Burn-side
Washington Heights
Roseland
Pullman
94
West Pullman
57
Riverdale
294
North Park
Albany Park
Lincoln Square
Portage Park
90
Irving Park
North Center
Lake View
Avondale
Roscoe Village
Her-mosa
Logan Square
94

IRVING PARK

ON CHICAGO'S NORTHWEST Side you'll find expansive green spaces, historic architecture, celebrated theaters, and plenty of independent, family owned and operated shops and eateries in the Irving Park and Portage Park neighborhoods. In Irving Park, see the Villa District's Victorian mansions and Arts & Crafts–style bungalows, some of which are listed on the National Register of Historic Places. In Portage Park, home to one of the largest Polish communities in the city, snap photos of the Portage Theater, one of the oldest movie houses in the Windy City (1920); see art produced by veterans at the National Veterans Art Museum; and shop, eat, and explore around the Six Corners District.

These family-centric, diverse neighborhoods have a plethora of year-round happenings worth exploring. For shopping, pop into Bob's Blues & Jazz Mart, Lincoln Antique Mall, and Rep Chi for unique items. Fresh fish is still being brought in daily at Hagen's Fish Shop, a family business since 1946, with one of the last surviving open-wood smokehouses. If you wander around long enough, you'll see something new and interesting.

Horner (Henry) Park

2741 W. Montrose Ave. • 773-478-3499 • www.chicagoparkdistrict.com

At nearly 58 acres—with baseball diamonds; football, softball, and soccer fields; basketball and tennis courts; and picnic areas—**Horner Park** is one of the best parks on the North Side. Well-located, at the intersection of Montrose and California, this massive green space hosts several family-friendly events, including movies in the park, running and fitness challenges, live music and theater, and holiday fun. Cultural and educational classes are available for all ages, including woodworking, toddler activities, and jazz ensembles, connecting folks to the community in a meaningful way.

Be sure to stroll through the **Nature Garden** and **Natural Area**, take your furry pals to the lively dog park, and burn energy at the playground. A large farmers market, supporting sustainable agriculture, runs from June through October in the northwest corner of the park, in front of the field house. Pick out a variety of fresh fruits and vegetables as well as other goods.

Horner (Henry) Park
(Courtesy of Victoria Kent)

Windy City Playhouse (Courtesy of Michael Brosilow)

Windy City Playhouse

3014 W. Irving Park Rd. • 773-891-8985 • www.windycityplayhouse.com

✔ Experience live, dynamic, and immersive theater at one of Chicago's top venues: **Windy City Playhouse**, a public-spirited professional theater that produces critically acclaimed shows. See an exciting, first-rate production in an intimate space designed to fully engage the audience. The flagship locale, which opened in 2015, has a modern, window-filled, front-of-house section with a charming cocktail bar and plenty of comfy lounge seating for socializing. It was designed by John Morris, the same celebrated theater architect who collaborated with **Steppenwolf Theater Company**, **Chicago Center for the Performing Arts**, **Lookingglass Theatre Company**, **Beverly Arts Center**, **Black Ensemble Theater Company**, and **Raven Theatre Chicago**. An outing here infuses Chicago theater history into the experience for guests.

For dining beforehand or afterward, and to make the most of the experience, visit nearby **Angelo's Wine Bar**, **Hearth and Crust**, **Old Irving Brewing Co.**, **Leader Bar Drafthouse and Eatery**, or **Raisu Sushi**.

Arun's Thai

4156 N. Kedzie Ave. • 773-539-1909
www.arunsthai.com

Whether you're looking for spicy BBQ fare, pub food, a Polish pierogi, Mexican cuisine, or Moroccan delights, palatable eateries abound in this area of the city. A well-reviewed local favorite, ideal for everyone in your family, is Arun's. Executive chef and owner Arun Sampanthavivat, born and raised in Thailand, works hard to make sure that every guest has an Instagram-worthy, delectable, and authentic meal. Elevated Thai dishes served in a warm and inviting atmosphere—complete with original Buddhist-inspired paintings, Thai silks and artifacts, and mahogany wood walls—transport you out of Chicago and into a different world where people slow down and connect with each other.

Select the prix-fixe nine-course menu and taste the best Arun's has to offer. Choose from either the sequential banquet or the family style banquet, posher than your traditional Thai street fare. A special vegan prix-fixe menu and an à la carte option are also available.

Arun's Thai (Courtesy of Wendy Altschuler)

Nearby Alternatives

Eat: Eris Brewery and Cider House

Located in historic **Old Irving Park**, Eris serves up hard cider, craft beer, and chow that caters to a wide range of diets (meat forward as well as meat, dairy, and gluten-free) where even the kids are considered. Women owned, Eris, which was once a Masonic Temple and a Korean church, also has a sizable patio.

4240 W. Irving Park Rd.
773-943-6200
www.erischicago.com

Discover: Irish American Heritage Center

Learn cultural history at the Irish American Heritage Center, where you can take part in festivals and events that focus on Irish music, theater, literature, dance, and language. Visit the art gallery, gift shop, library, museum, and traditional pub, and listen to the Irish heritage singers.

4626 N. Knox Ave.
773-282-7035
www.irish-american.org

Play: Portage Park

An intricate gateway entrance welcomes families to Portage Park, a 38-acre green space with multi-age programs, sports fields, a playground, a dog park, a boxing center, a bike path, a senior center, natural walking areas, a cultural arts building, and an Olympic-sized swimming pool. It's an urban oasis for all.

4100 N. Long Ave.
773-685-7235
www.chicagoparkdistrict.com

Shop: Polonia Bookstore

For something newfangled but with a strong sense of place, visit a local bookstore. Touted as America's oldest Polish American bookshop, Polonia has been an area staple since 1969. Peruse Polish literature, English-language texts, Polish newspapers and magazines, or a variety of greeting cards. There's a children's section and café as well.

4759 N. Milwaukee Ave.
773-481-6968
www.poloniabookstorechicago.com

Trip Planning

Portage Park Chamber of Commerce

773-777-2020
www.portageparkchamber.org

294
94
Edison Park
Rogers park
West Ridge
Norwood Park
Forest Glen
North Park
Edge-water
Andersonville
O'Hare International Airport
190
90
Jefferson Park
Lincoln Square
Albany Park
Uptown
O'Hare
Portage Park
Irving Park
Wrigleyville
Dunning
North Center
Lake View
Northalsted
294
Avondale
Roscoe Village
Mont-clare
Belmont Cragin
Her-mosa
Logan Square
Lincoln Park
94
Old Town
Wicker Park
Gold Coast
West Town
River North
Magnificent Mile
Austin
Humboldt Park
Ukrainian Village
Streeterville
West Garfield Park
East Garfield Park
West Loop
Near West Side
Loop
290
290
90
South Loop
North Lawndale
Pilsen
Chinatown
Little Village
South Lawndale
55
McKinley Park
Bridge-port
Armour Square
Douglas
Oak-land
Fuller Park
294
Back of the Yards
Bronzeville
Grand Boulevard
Kenwood
Washington Park
Hyde Park
94
Engle-wood
Woodlawn
Greater Grand Crossing
Chatham
Avalon Park
94
Burn-side
Washington Heights
Roseland
Pullman
Morgan Park
94
West Pullman
57
Riverdale
294
Andersonville
Lincoln Square
Albany Park
Uptown
Wrigleyville
90
Irving Park
North Center
Lake View
Northalsted
Avondale
Roscoe Village
Her-mosa
Logan Square
Lincoln Park
94
Old Town
Wicker Park
Gold Coast
West Town
River North
Ukrainian Village

ROSCOE VILLAGE

KNOWN AS THE "village within the city," Roscoe Village is loved by Chicagoans not only for its parks, brick homes, and quirky retro feel, but also for its independent boutiques, lively arts scene, brunch spots, and nightlife.

Eclectic shops like Shangri-La Vintage, a mecca for old-school fashions; Praha, with unique antique furniture; Little Threads, a neighborhood kids' store; and Twinkle Twinkle Little One, a one-stop shop for all-things baby; provide sightseers with inimitable shopping experiences. Learn at August House Chicago, an exhibit gallery that offers painting and drawing classes for every age; see street art via the Lakeview Public Art Program; and see works created by talented artists at Cornelia Arts Building. Popular eateries include family-friendly Orange on Roscoe; Kitsch'n on Roscoe, a long-standing joint with funky décor; Lucy's Café, for vegetarian and vegan fare; The Bad Apple; and Savannah Supper Club, specializing in Southern dishes. For nightlife, check out music-forward Constellation; Village Tap, a gastropub; Cody's Public House, a dog-friendly watering hole; Beat Kitchen, for live music and stand-up comedy; and family-owned Roscoe Village Pub, with an outdoor patio.

Roscoe Village Farmers Market

John Elementary School:
3149 N. Wolcott Ave.
773-472-7171
www.lakeviewroscoevillage.org

✓ Enjoy outdoor festivals and community events like **Retro on Roscoe**, **Lakeview Roscoe Village Restaurant Week**, **Spring Wine Walk**, **Belmont Bunny Hop**, and **Ribfest** in Roscoe Village.

Another option is to simply bring your family and friends and wander around the **Roscoe Village Farmers Market** to get a real feel of the neighborhood. From June to October, you'll find not only fresh fruits and vegetables, but also just-baked breads and pastries, cheeses, and honey. Shop for coffee, house plants, and handmade soaps; listen to live music; and treat the kids to ice cream. Your visit will support an independent market that does much for the community and surrounding areas by cultivating sustainability through access to local and seasonal food sources as well as elevating small businesses within Roscoe Village. Plus, it's such a treat to enjoy a pleasant Chicago day at a spot where neighbors and visitors mingle and mix.

Roscoe Village Farmers Market (Courtesy of Friends of Lakeview)

Roscoe Books (Courtesy of Wendy Altschuler)

Roscoe Books

2142 W. Roscoe St. • 773-857-2676 • www.roscoebooks.com

✔ Many of Chicago's neighborhoods feel like small towns in a big city. There's just something about exploring the shops, eating in the restaurants, and attending an event that makes you appreciate this vibrant community. A local bookstore is one of those businesses that brings people together, whether you're a long-time resident or visiting for the weekend.

The storefront of **Roscoe Books** brightens up the street with its oval green sign hanging above a book-filled window display. Inside, you'll find a distinctive children's section that beckons littles to wander in and sit on a beanbag with a new picture book. Adults will value the thoughtful staff picks, each with a detailed, hand-written description; engaging book clubs; and author events and book signings. Weekly story times are ideal for parents who want to socialize and create a network around child rearing. You won't regret stepping inside this warm and welcoming home-grown space.

Le Sud

2301 W. Roscoe St. • 773-857-1985
www.lesudchicago.com

In the Windy City's warm-weather months, cafés flow out onto the sidewalks, inviting wanderers to linger a bit longer. Patrons at **Le Sud**, a Mediterranean-inspired café with simple yet flavorful ingredients, can enjoy patio or rooftop dining. Should you want to eat inside, however, the bright ambience is just as inviting. Tastes of France, Italy, and Spain are woven throughout the menu, including on the extensive wine list. From monthly wine tasting events highlighting global varietals, to private dining, to a kids' menu, there's something for everyone.

Make a reservation for the sought-after corner Table23, the best table in the house, and Le Sud will donate 23 percent of your dining bill to Audubon or Lane Tech Schools, Common Pantry, Roscoe Village Neighbors, or Lakeview Roscoe Village Chamber of Commerce organizations. It's worth noting that Le Sud's sister restaurant, **Koi Fine Asian Cuisine & Lounge**, located in Evanston, is also an excellent choice.

Le Sud (Courtesy of Wendy Altschuler)

Nearby Alternatives

Play: Hamlin Park

Hamlin Park, set in the North Center community, offers nine acres of family-friendly fun. In addition to the swimming pool, sports fields, playground, and dog park, activities like yoga, kids' fitness classes, weightlifting, boxing, volleyball, tot and teen modules, dance acts, and special events like the **Boxing Show** engage visitors.

3035 N. Hoyne Ave.
312-742-7785
www.chicagoparkdistrict.com

Play: Waveland Bowl

The largest bowling alley in Chicago, Waveland Bowl, locally owned and operated since 1959, is the place to go for classic family-friendly fun. Munch on hot dogs, burgers, and pizza at **Alley Dogs**. Check out the **Cosmic Bowling**, with black lights and energetic music, arcade, and billiards room.

3700 N. Western Ave.
773-472-5900
www.wavelandbowl.com

Shop: Building Blocks Toy Store

For a special surprise, take your kids to this toy shop full of playthings for all ages, where you can find arts and crafts supplies, bathtub fun, action figures, fidget spinners, travel games, science and nature items, toys for kids with special needs, musical toys, masks, and more.

3306 N. Lincoln Ave.
773-525-6200
www.buildingblockstoys.com

Play: Windy City Ninjas

Calling all *American Ninja Warrior* aficionados: fly, climb walls, build strength, and learn something new at Windy City Ninjas, a family-friendly fitness facility with structured classes for kids ages 2 to 16, as well as for adults, plus an age-appropriate open gym.

2500 W. Bradley Pl.
773-886-1996
www.windycityninjas.com

Trip Planning

Lakeview Roscoe Village Chamber of Commerce

1409 W. Addison St.
773-472-7171
www.lakeviewroscoevillage.org

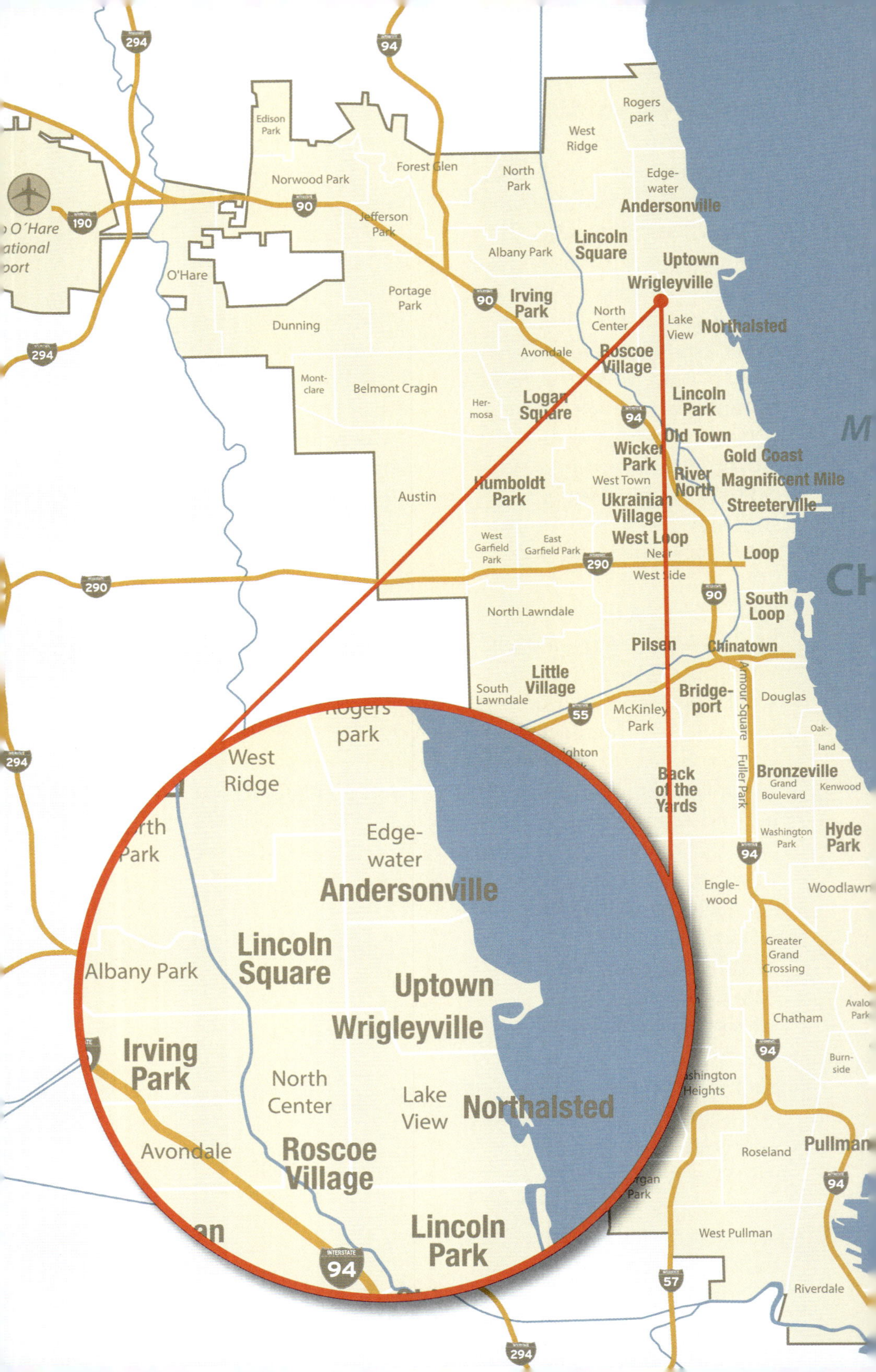

Edison Park
Norwood Park
Forest Glen
North Park
West Ridge
Rogers park
Edge-water
Andersonville
Lincoln Square
Uptown
Wrigleyville
Jefferson Park
Albany Park
O'Hare
Portage Park
Irving Park
North Center
Lake View
Northalsted
Dunning
Avondale
Roscoe Village
Mont-clare
Belmont Cragin
Her-mosa
Logan Square
Lincoln Park
Old Town
Wicker Park
Gold Coast
River North
Magnificent Mile
West Town
Humboldt Park
Austin
Ukrainian Village
Streeterville
West Garfield Park
East Garfield Park
West Loop
Near West Side
Loop
South Loop
North Lawndale
Pilsen
Chinatown
Little Village
South Lawndale
Bridge-port
McKinley Park
Armour Square
Douglas
Oak-land
Back of the Yards
Fuller Park
Bronzeville
Grand Boulevard
Kenwood
Washington Park
Hyde Park
Engle-wood
Woodlawn
Greater Grand Crossing
Chatham
Avalon Park
Burn-side
Washington Heights
Roseland
Pullman
Morgan Park
West Pullman
Riverdale
O'Hare International Airport
294
94
90
190
290
55
57

WRIGLEYVILLE

FROM LOVABLE LOSERS to World Series champs, the Chicago Cubs entertain crowds at historic Wrigley Field. Situated right in the heart of Wrigleyville, within the Lakeview neighborhood on Chicago's North Side, this active MLB ballpark is the second oldest in America behind Boston's Fenway Park. Visitors can watch a game behind the diamond or via Wrigley Rooftops, an inimitable and inclusive food and drinks experience where you can cheer on the Cubs at one of the surrounding 11 rooftops along Waveland and Sheffield avenues.

Catch Cubs fever just outside of the Friendly Confines, where sports fans of all ages can swing a bat or play in the arcade at Sluggers. Stock up on souvenirs in one of the many t-shirt and tchotchke shops or buy goods from a street vendor during games. For the full experience, pop into one of the several sports bars, beer gardens, or eateries in Wrigleyville: Murphy's Bleachers, Cloud Cookie, Smoke Daddy BBQ, Big Star, Do-Rite Donuts & Chicken, Wrigleyville Dogs, Swift & Sons Tavern, the Cubby Bear, Happy Camper, or Lucky's Sandwich Company.

Wrigley Field

1060 W. Addison St. • 773-404-CUBS • www.cubs.com

Begin your adventure at **Wrigley Field**, built in 1914, for a rowdy game where you can bellow out your order for beer, peanuts, or hot dogs as vendors roam the aisles. See the famous ivy-covered walls in the outfield and the old-school manual scoreboard.

Ballpark tours, fun for learning about over a century of baseball history, will also delve into the Cubs' journey leading up to the 2016 World Series Championship, ending a 108-year drought. Make sure your guide tells you about the Curse of the Billy Goat. Non–game day tours include visits to the press box, bleachers, clubhouse, dugout, and field.

Pro Tip: Leave your car and take public transportation. The Addison stop on the CTA Red Line is a half block from Wrigley Field. Ride shares are an option; however, be aware of surge pricing. If you must drive, you'll find locals on the street hawking residential parking spots.

Wrigley Field (Courtesy of Wendy Altschuler)

Gallagher Way (Courtesy of @tequilagraphics, Choose Chicago)

Gallagher Way

3637 N. Clark St. • 773-388-8260 • www.gallagherway.com

✓ Whether you're visiting for a Cubs game or just want to explore Wrigleyville, **Gallagher Way**, located next to Wrigley Field, brings locals and vacationers together all year round. A massive upgrade to the city following the 2016 World Series win, this open-air destination, which includes the well-designed **Hotel Zachary**, is a green-space gem.

Ticket holders can visit before or after a game to enjoy game broadcasts, live music, shopping, and dining. Families can play catch in the grass, lounge in the sun, or eat at **Budweiser Brickhouse Tavern** or **Jeni's Wrigleyville**.

In addition to baseball games, you can see an outdoor film, join a fitness class, listen to live music from emerging artists as well as seasoned pros, and shop at the **Farmers Market** during the warmer months. In the chillier season, stroll **Christkindlmarket**, go ice skating, visit **Santa's Workshop**, see a holiday flick, or celebrate Hanukkah, all with a close-up view of Wrigley Field.

Uncommon Ground

3800 N. Clark St. • 773-929-3680 • www.uncommonground.com

✓ For something a little different from what you might expect, dine at Uncommon Ground, home of the first certified organic brewery in Illinois, **Greenstar Brewing**. The second Edgewater location is where you'll find the first certified organic rooftop farm in the US, complete with honeybee hives, where produce grown is used in both eateries. Uncommon Ground is open for brunch and dinner, and you can enjoy healthy options that will satisfy everyone in your group—carnivores and vegans, kids and grandparents.

In keeping with the restaurant's "eat, drink, look, listen" ethos, patrons can hear live music from local and national artists during dinner shows each week. Notable past performers include Jeff Buckley, Train, and Chris Shiflett (Foo Fighters). Uncommon Ground also supports a diverse range of home-grown artists—see original works during art openings. Leaders in the farm-to-table movement, Uncommon Ground has been independently owned and operated for over 30 years. Try the contemporary comfort cuisine before heading out for more exploring.

Uncommon Ground
(Courtesy of Uncommon Ground)

Nearby Alternatives

Discover: Alta Vista Terrace District

Venture a couple blocks north of **Wrigley Field** and you'll discover European-style row houses built in 1903 and 1904 by real-estate developer Samuel Eberly Gross. As you wander down the one-block section of the Alta Vista Terrace District, where 40 historic row homes sit, you'll feel like you're exploring a secret pocket of London.

3800 block of North Alta Vista Terrace

Discover: Mercury Theater Chicago

Near Wrigley Field in the **Southport Corridor**, where you'll find charming boutiques, eateries, and homes, the 280-seat **Mercury Theater** offers something for all ages. Next door, the **Venus Cabaret Theater** offers a full lineup of entertainment, from comedy to live music, open-mic nights, variety shows, and karaoke.

3745 N. Southport Ave.
773-360-7365
www.mercurytheaterchicago.com

Discover: Music Box Theater

A few steps from Mercury Theater Chicago, Music Box Theater is a haven for lovers of independent, foreign, cult, and classic films. This historic movie house, which opened in 1929, shows midnight movies, weekend matinees, and films that center on a theme. The lounge and garden are fun meet-up spaces for after the show.

3733 N. Southport Ave.
773-871-6604
www.musicboxtheater.com

Discover: Metro Chicago

With theater and film covered, another venue that has been going strong since 1982 is the Metro. Listen to a variety of musical genres, appropriate for a range of ages, in an intimate setting. This concert hall has served as an incubator of sorts for emerging artists who "make it big."

3730 N. Clark St.
773-549-4140
www.metrochicago.com

Trip Planning

Lakeview East Chamber of Commerce

3138 N. Broadway
773-348-8608
www.wrigleyvillechicago.org

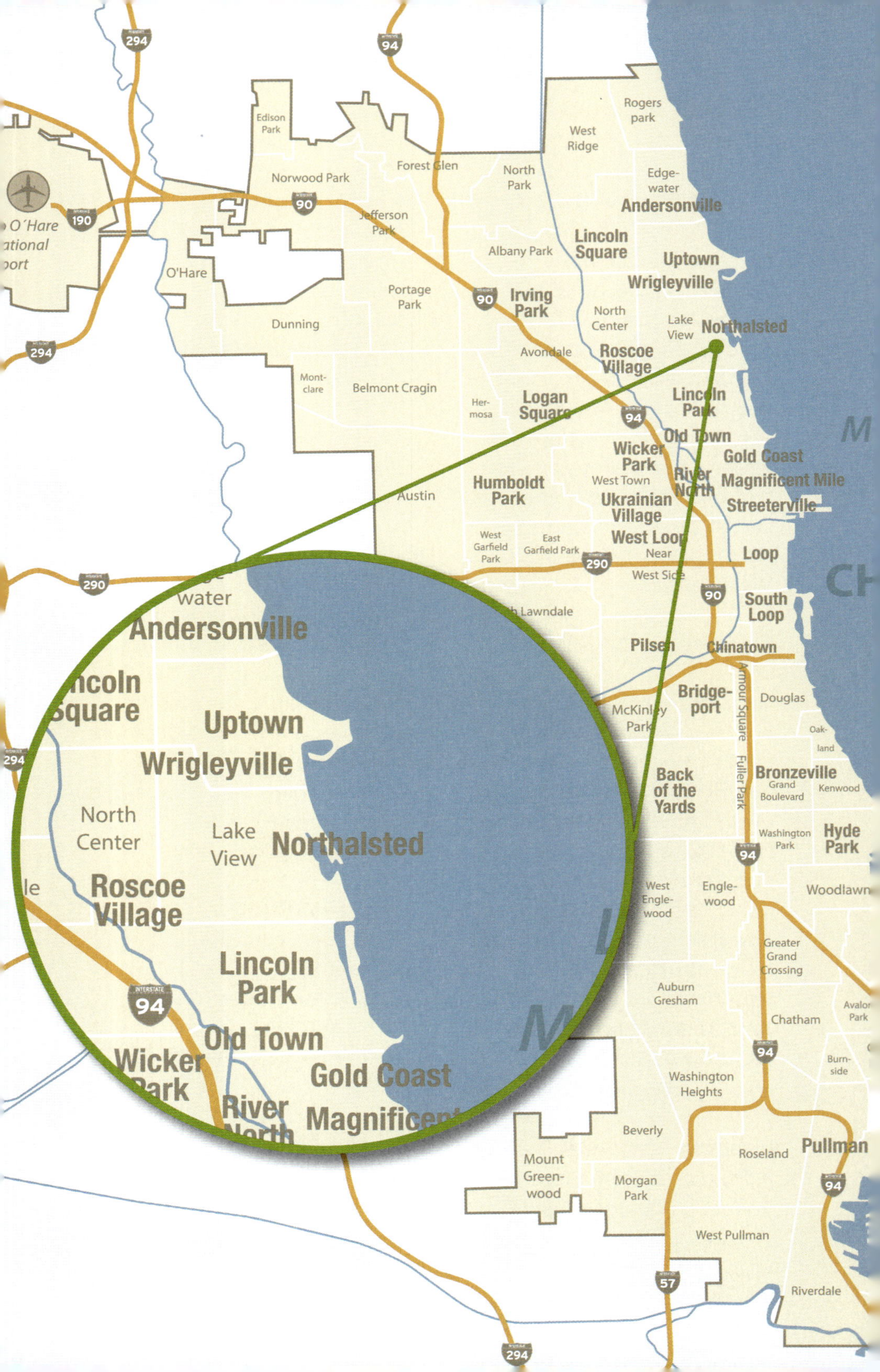

O´Hare
ational
port
Edison Park
Norwood Park
Forest Glen
North Park
West Ridge
Rogers park
Edgewater
Andersonville
Jefferson Park
Albany Park
Lincoln Square
Uptown
Wrigleyville
O'Hare
Portage Park
Irving Park
North Center
Lake View
Northalsted
Dunning
Avondale
Roscoe Village
Montclare
Belmont Cragin
Hermosa
Logan Square
Lincoln Park
Old Town
Wicker Park
Gold Coast
Austin
Humboldt Park
West Town
River North
Magnificent Mile
Ukrainian Village
Streeterville
West Garfield Park
East Garfield Park
West Loop
Near West Side
Loop
South Loop
Lawndale
Pilsen
Chinatown
Bridgeport
McKinley Park
Douglas
Armour Square
Fuller Park
Oakland
Back of the Yards
Bronzeville
Grand Boulevard
Kenwood
Washington Park
Hyde Park
West Englewood
Englewood
Woodlawn
Greater Grand Crossing
Auburn Gresham
Chatham
Avalon Park
Burnside
Washington Heights
Beverly
Roseland
Pullman
Mount Greenwood
Morgan Park
West Pullman
Riverdale

NORTHALSTED

TEN PAIRS OF 25-foot rainbow pylons with bronze biographical memorial markers honoring notable people in the LGBTQ+ community mark Northalsted, or Boystown, the first recognized gay village in America. Nestled in Lakeview east of Wrigleyville, the Legacy Walk, an outdoor exhibit, is an internationally recognized historic landmark that sees 1.5 million visitors per year. You'll notice 14 Chicago Rainbow Pride Crosswalks, making the Windy City home to the longest pride promenade in the world. Another first-of-its-kind site is the Center on Halsted, an eco-friendly LEEDS-certified community complex with programming for all ages, from teens to seniors. From colossal street festivals and parades like Northalsted Market Days, Chicago Pride Fest and Parade, and Northalsted Halloween Parade, to exciting happenings like Northalsted Soup & Sip, Taste of Northalsted, and Lakeview Pup Crawl, there's always something going on.

A welcoming and accepting milieu for folks of all ages, this vibrant North Side district is well known for its nightlife (Kit Kat Lounge and Supper Club is a must), many theaters, comedy clubs, coffee shops, eateries, funky boutiques, and community celebrations.

Blue Man Group

3133 N. Halsted St. • 800-258-3626 • www.blueman.com

✔ Blue Man Group at **Briar Street Theater**, a space built in 1901 that was once used as the stables for Marshall Field's horses, is an incredible strobe-light-filled experience certain to be a highlight of your time in Chicago. This long-running spectacle, where three cobalt-blue men dressed in black make you laugh, dance, and clap through on-topic and trending comedy, music, and immersive audience experiences, has been in operation since 1997. Teens love the pop culture references, children stare in awe at the drums full of neon paint that splatter in the air when beat, and adults dig the on-stage three-piece rock band that jams throughout the show. The performers don't speak, but their body language and facial expressions tell a story in bite-sized vignettes. Be prepared for something artistic, avant-garde even, and choose the "poncho seats" up front if you dare.

Blue Man Group, Chicago
(Courtesy of Kyle Flubacker)

Courtesy of Windy City Sweets

Windy City Sweets

3308 N. Broadway • 773-477-6100 • www.windycitysweets.com

✓ Pop into **Windy City Sweets**, a traditional candy store with chocolate treats, handmade fudge, gourmet nuts, gummi candy, and frozen desserts in cone, malt, sundae, sorbet, or smoothie form. Open since 1983, this well-loved North Side shop has over 1,200 distinctive sweet treats. Gift tins and baskets are available, which are perfect for group picnicking. Signature chocolate blends are handmade in the store every week. Look for something special, nostalgic, and not found anywhere else. Chocolate-covered fruit, gourmet truffles, caramel nut patties, and chocolate covered s'mores are fan favorites. You can just smell it, right?

With sugary goodies in hand, walk two blocks northwest to nearby **Wendt Playlot Park**, a small neighborhood playground. **Gill Park**, which is eight blocks north, is much larger and has turf climbing mounds, playground equipment, fitness programs, and an indoor swimming pool. Venture east and watch the boats on **Lake Michigan's Belmont Harbor**.

Chicago Diner

3411 N. Halsted St.
773-935-6696 • www.veggiediner.com

✓ Meat free since '83, Lakeview's Chicago Diner is not only one of the best vegetarian and vegan restaurants in the city, but also one of the coolest. With vintage signs, booth seating, and classic American fare, this eatery offers up Midwestern comfort picks like country-fried steak, Ruebens, biscuits and gravy, pot pies, burgers, and chicken fingers for the kids—all without the meat. Try one of their famous vegan milkshakes and be sure to leave room for a house-made dessert. Reservations are encouraged, parking is limited, and outdoor seating is available (and lovely). Should you want to try your hand at cooking some of the café specialties, you can purchase one of their two cookbooks and create meals at home.

The Chicago Diner gives back to multiple nonprofits, including animal rescues and sanctuaries, so you can feel good knowing that a portion of what you pay goes toward worthy causes.

Chicago Diner (Courtesy of Del Nakamura, northalsted.com)

Nearby Alternatives

Play: Trickery

With its storefront location visible to onlookers, this intimate performance-art theater is quite unique. See if your brain can square the tricks your eyes are witnessing. Snap photos before the show, ideal for ages 12 and up, while sitting on the red couch under the "Hoppy the Psychic Wonder Bunny" artwork. Magic.

3453 N. Halsted St.
312-566-8061
www.trickerychicago.com

Discover: The Annoyance Theater

With a little something for everyone, the Annoyance Theater showcases improv comedy, original plays, musicals, sketch comedy, and more. See big national acts as well as local talent at this effervescent playhouse. And, with classes and the **Comedy Conservatory**, you can get comprehensive skill-based instruction as well.

851 W. Belmont, Floor 2
773-697-9693
www.theannoyance.com

Shop: Unabridged Bookstore

Regularly included on "best of" lists throughout the city, Unabridged Bookstore has been a neighborhood staple for over 40 years. Not only are staff recommendations plentiful and handwritten, but there's also a sizable children's section and travel room. Poetry and fiction lovers will be pleased as well.

3251 N. Broadway
773-883-9119
www.unabridgedbookstore.com

Eat: Wood

In the heart of the Northalsted neighborhood sits Wood, an elevated-yet-casual restaurant with executive chef Devin Kreller (North Pond) captaining the ship. Families love the shareable house-made pastas, wood-fired flatbreads, and seasonal salads. Named after the owner's father, who was a woodworker, Wood has earned the Michelin Bib Gourmand accolade six times.

3335 N. Halsted St.
773-935-9663
www.woodchicago.com

Trip Planning

Northalsted Business Alliance

3656 N. Halsted St.
773-883-0500
www.northalsted.com

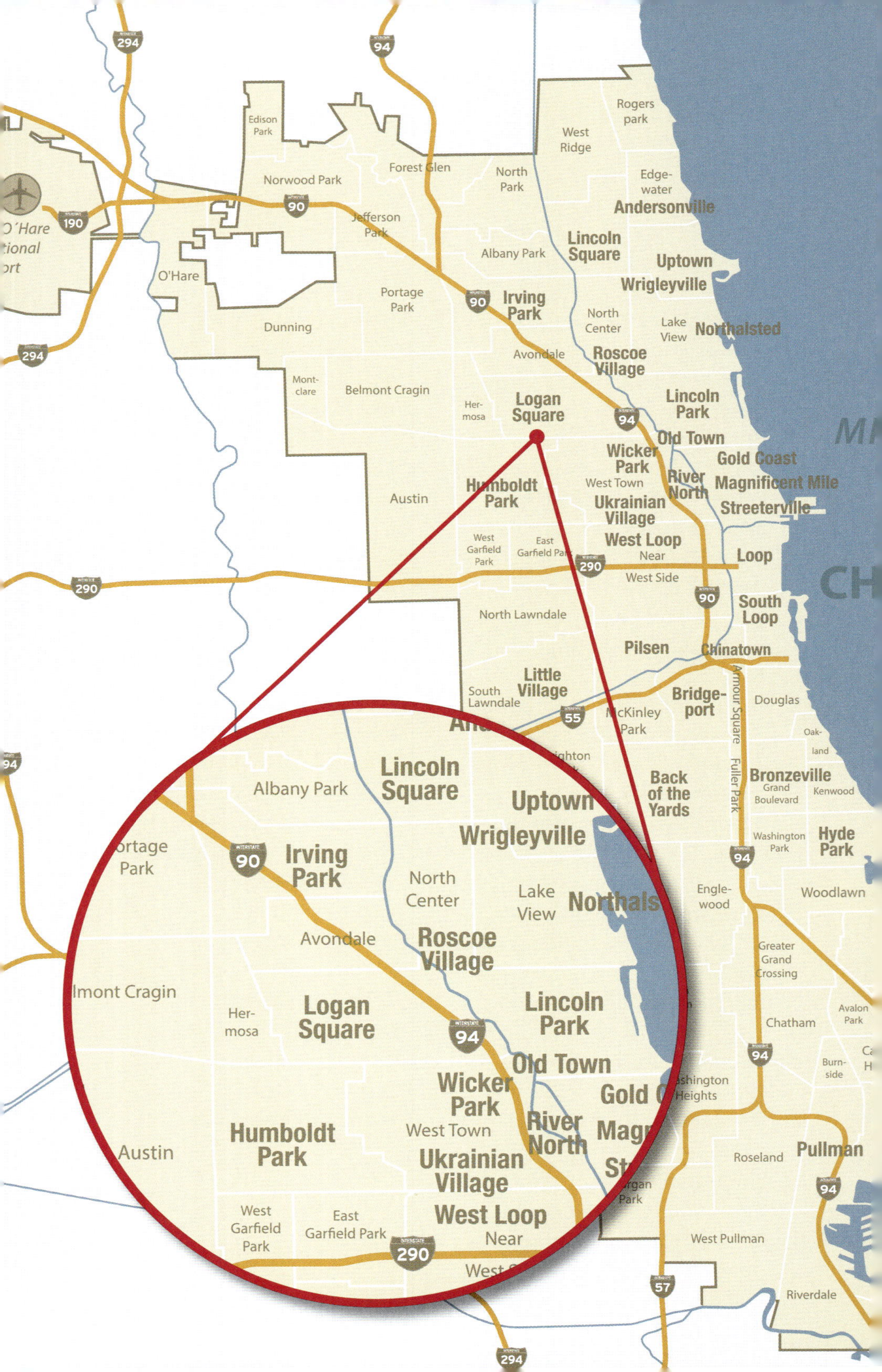
Rogers park
West Ridge
Edgewater
Andersonville
Edison Park
Norwood Park
Forest Glen
North Park
Jefferson Park
Albany Park
Lincoln Square
Uptown
O'Hare
Portage Park
Irving Park
North Center
Wrigleyville
Lake View
Northalsted
Dunning
Avondale
Roscoe Village
Montclare
Belmont Cragin
Hermosa
Logan Square
Lincoln Park
Old Town
Wicker Park
West Town
Gold Coast
River North
Magnificent Mile
Austin
Humboldt Park
Ukrainian Village
Streeterville
West Garfield Park
East Garfield Park
West Loop
Near West Side
Loop
South Loop
North Lawndale
Pilsen
Chinatown
South Lawndale
Little Village
McKinley Park
Bridgeport
Armour Square
Douglas
Oakland
Back of the Yards
Fuller Park
Bronzeville
Grand Boulevard
Kenwood
Washington Park
Hyde Park
Englewood
Woodlawn
Greater Grand Crossing
Chatham
Avalon Park
Burnside
Washington Heights
Roseland
Pullman
Morgan Park
West Pullman
Riverdale
294
94
90
190
290
55
57

LOGAN SQUARE

THE COMMUNITY AREA of Logan Square, which includes Belmont Gardens, Bucktown, Kosciuszko Park, Palmer Square, and Logan Square neighborhoods, is home to wide boulevards, handsome greystone and bungalow-style dwellings, and age-old churches. A walkable commercial corridor along the three-way intersection of Milwaukee Avenue, Logan Boulevard, and Kedzie Boulevard has a plethora of eateries, theaters, bakeries, and boutiques.

From stellar brunch spots (Lula Café, Reno Chicago, Longman & Eagle, Same Day Café, 90 Miles Cuban Café, Bang Bang Pie & Biscuits), to the award-winning Logan Square Farmers Market, to dozens of coffee shops (Passion House, New Wave Coffee, Sip of Hope Coffee Bar, Gaslight Coffee Roasters), to a fun nightlife scene (Emporium, Logan Arcade, the Owl, Midlane Esports), to the three-day Logan Square Arts Festival, you'll find it easy to whittle hours away.

A long-established Latinx community has welcomed new denizens who have changed the landscape of the neighborhood, so the indie attitude perseveres in this society full of artists (Galerie F), comedians (Lincoln Lodge), musicians (Concord Music Hall, Rosa's Lounge, the Whistler), and creative entrepreneurs.

Palmer Square Park

2200 N. Kedzie Ave. • 312-742-7535 • www.chicagoparkdistrict.com

Begin your adventure at **Logan Square Park**, where you'll find the Illinois **Centennial Monument**, **Comfort Station**, and **Logan Square Farmers Market**. Travel on foot—or borrow a Divvy rental bike—down North Kedzie Boulevard, past **Logan Square Auditorium** and the well-loved **City Lit Books**, to Palmer Square Park. Little kids crawl all over the **Velveteen Rabbit** play area, fitness-minded folks run around the track, and multi-generational families spend the afternoon picnicking in the grass at this nearly eight-acre park.

In the 1880s and early 1900s grand homes were developed around these historic boulevards. Should time and energy allow, bring your family farther south on North Humboldt Boulevard, past the popular **Parson's Chicken and Fish**, the **Yellow Brick Road** (where Lyman Frank Baum wrote *The Wonderful Wizard of Oz* at 1667 N. Humboldt Blvd.), and the *There's No Place Like Home* mosaic. End at Humboldt Park.

Palmer Square Park (Courtesy of Scott Altschuler)

The 606 (Courtesy of Wendy Altschuler)

The 606

1610 W. Bloomingdale Ave.
312-742-4622 • www.the606.org

Whether you like to bike, roller skate, or run, visit the 606—the **Bloomington Trail**. Much like New York City's High Line, what was once an abandoned rail line has been transformed into an elevated 2.7-mile-long park and path traveling over four neighborhoods—Wicker Park, Bucktown, Humboldt Park, and Logan Square—situated between Ashland and Ridgeway, with 12 access points every quarter mile. The **Exelon Observatory**, shaped with steel notched edges, frames sunsets on the first day of each season. The designers worked with **Adler Planetarium** astronomers to ensure that spectators would be able to stargaze.

This green space not only weds nature and science, but also nature and culture through art displays, community events, musical performances, and stewardship activities. Visit **Julie De Burgos Park**, featuring a climbing web; **Damen Arts Plaza**, with rotating art; **Park No. 567**, known for Jeff Zimmermann's "ConAgra" mural; and **Walsh Park**, with a playground and dog park.

Osteria Langhe

2824 W. Armitage Ave. • 773-661-1582 • www.osterialanghe.com

✓ What really sets this restaurant apart from all the other Italian eateries in the city—beyond the locally-sourced fare, wines and recipes from Italy's Piemonte region, charming interior, and seasonal patio—is the sense of place and purpose created by owner Aldo Zaninotto and executive chef Cameron Grant, both of whom are customer-facing—neither hides in the back out of view. If you want to compliment the chef, you can shake Grant's hand. If you desire a northern Italian wine recommendation from a passionate expert, Zaninotto is there. Since 2014, Osteria Langhe has been a city staple for its ingredient-focused fare and contribution to the Slow Food movement, said to have been born in the Piemonte region. Order a seasonal risotto or house-made ravioli if on the menu, and be sure to ask for the wine list, which is full of delightful red, white, and sparkling options curated by the owner himself.

Osteria Langhe (Courtesy of Rachel Bires)

Nearby Alternatives

Discover: Illinois Centennial Monument

This 67-foot-tall eagle-capped Doric column overlooks Logan Square Boulevard Historic District's Logan Square Park. The monument marks the edge of Chicago's Park and Boulevard System, which includes 8 parks, 19 boulevards, and 6 squares that stretch over 1,700 acres of greenery along 26 miles of roadways.

3200 W. Logan Blvd.
www.chicagomonuments.org

Discover: The Logan Theater

In 1915, the Logan Theater was a single-screen cinema. Surviving 30 years of neighborhood transformation, this family institution stayed open. See the restored stained-glass arch, marble walls, Art Deco details, and modern updates as you visit the concessions, box office, and lobby. Movie tickets are offered at family-friendly rates.

2646 N. Milwaukee Ave.
773-342-5555
www.thelogantheater.com

Play: Hairpin Arts Center

This nonprofit multidisciplinary arts organization promotes cultural opportunities through events, exhibits, educational classes, and performances. Located in the historic Morris B. Sachs building and managed by the Logan Square Chamber of Arts, the center is home to musical and visual arts performances as well as cross-disciplinary exchanges.

2810 W. Milwaukee Ave.
773-489-3222
www.hairpinartscenter.org

Discover: Comfort Station

During the 1920s, comfort stations, or warming buildings, were built along transit lines across Chicago's Park Boulevard System. The Tudor-style Logan Square Comfort Station is one of only two that remain. The building was being used as a tool shed when Logan Square Preservation restored the building in the early 2000s and turned it into a community-driven multimedia public arts enclave where you can see local art.

2579 N. Milwaukee Ave.
773-981-5291
www.comfortstationlogansquare.org

Trip Planning

Logan Square Chamber of Commerce

2808 N. Milwaukee Ave.
773-489-3222
www.loganchamber.org

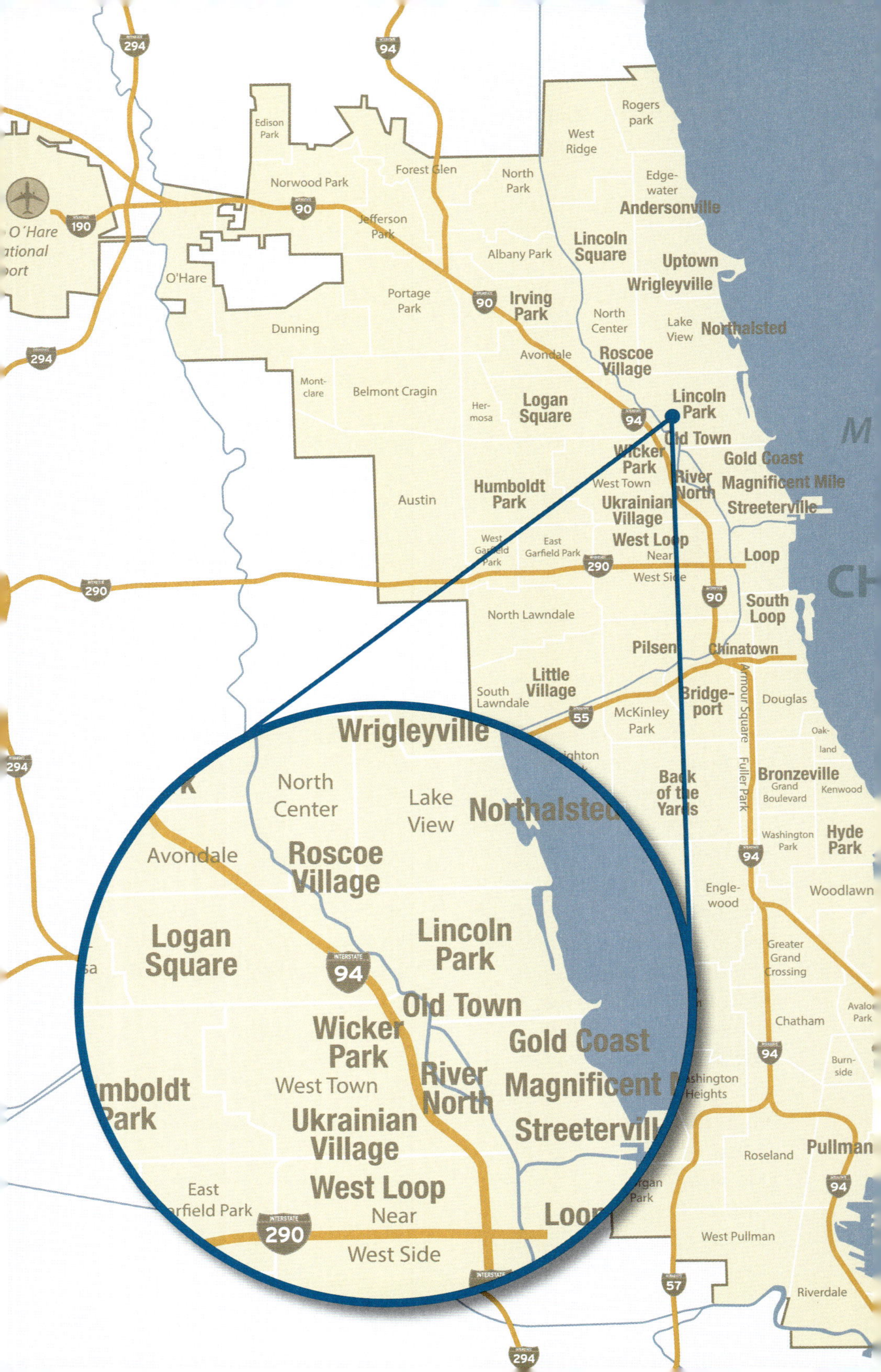

294
94
Edison Park
Rogers park
West Ridge
Forest Glen
North Park
Norwood Park
Edge-water
Andersonville
90
Jefferson Park
190
O'Hare
Lincoln Square
Albany Park
Uptown
Wrigleyville
Portage Park
90
Irving Park
North Center
Lake View
Northalsted
Dunning
294
Avondale
Roscoe Village
Mont-clare
Belmont Cragin
Her-mosa
Logan Square
94
Lincoln Park
Old Town
Wicker Park
Gold Coast
River North
Magnificent Mile
Humboldt Park
West Town
Austin
Ukrainian Village
Streeterville
West Loop
West Garfield Park
East Garfield Park
Near West Side
290
Loop
290
90
South Loop
North Lawndale
Pilsen
Chinatown
Little Village
South Lawndale
Bridge-port
Armour Square
Douglas
McKinley Park
55
Oak-land
Back of the Yards
Fuller Park
Bronzeville
Grand Boulevard
Kenwood
294
Washington Park
Hyde Park
94
Engle-wood
Woodlawn
Greater Grand Crossing
Chatham
94
Burn-side
Roseland
Pullman
94
West Pullman
57
Riverdale
294

LINCOLN PARK

JUST BECAUSE THE city of big shoulders is a large metropolis of 2.75 million people doesn't mean that there's a lack of access to nature and the outdoors. Lincoln Park, situated on Chicago's North Side, is not only one of the area's most affluent neighborhoods, but also home to the largest park in the Windy City. Learn about the wild world around you and stroll through manicured gardens, have a Zen moment at a veiled lily pond, breathe deep inside a historic botanical garden and a nature museum, enjoy sweeping city views along the Lakefront Trail, and wander through the oldest free zoo in the country.

A sandy beach is perfect for family picnicking, the General Ulysses S. Grant and Abraham Lincoln statues are great for history buffs, and foodies will love all the Michelin-rated and recommended restaurants: Galit, Alinea, Adobo Grill, BOKA, Esmé, Twin Anchors, Avli Taverna, Juno, and North Pond. The park is full of families, working professionals, and students, and there's a myriad of things to do, see, and explore for folks of all ages.

Lincoln Park Zoo

2400 N. Cannon Dr. • 312-742-2000 • www.lpzoo.org

This free urban zoo, created in 1868, is open every day of the year. See nearly 200 species from around the globe, including lions, black bears, camels, monkeys, chimpanzees, rhinoceroses, giraffes, zebras, gorillas, and polar bears. Explore the African Journey, Arctic Tundra, Penguin Cove, Bird House, Macaque Forest, Family Children's Zoo, Seal Pool, Lion House, Small Mammal-Reptile House, Primate House, Center for African Apes, and the Farm-in-the-Zoo areas. Ride the carousel and the train. Dine at the **Park Place Café** or the **Patio at Café Brauer**.

Don't miss wandering through the **Lincoln Park Conservatory**, a Victorian glass greenhouse with palms, orchids, ferns, and flowers. East of the conservatory sits the Alfred Caldwell Lily Pool. On the south end of the zoo, you'll find the Nature Boardwalk, an urban oasis for flora and fauna; the honeycomb Education Pavilion, a top spot for photographs; and **Green City Market**, an outdoor sustainable food marketplace with educational programming.

Lincoln Park Zoo (Courtesy of Wendy Altschuler)

Courtesy of Wendy Altschuler

Peggy Notebaert Nature Museum

2430 N. Cannon Dr. • 773-755-5100 • www.naturemuseum.org

✓ North of the zoo, sandwiched between **North Pond Nature Sanctuary and Diversey Harbor**—near Theater on the Lake and the Lakefront Trail—you'll find the **Chicago Academy of Sciences's** Peggy Notebaert Nature Museum. Popular with visitors of all ages, this accessible and affordable museum engages visitors with nature and science through immersive demonstrations, energetic events, and educational curriculums. As you wander through the informative areas, including the live Butterfly Haven and the outdoor **Nature Trails**, you'll learn about diverse ecosystems and the ecological history of the Illinois region. Keep an eye out for nature-inspired art, watch scientists working in the **Look-In Lab**, and visit the toddler-appropriate play spaces. Take part in one of the many programs, including butterfly releases, yoga classes, or animal feedings. From exhibits that delve into weather and climate, rivers and marshes, and animal taxidermy to displays on conservation research and community science, a visit here is a must.

The J. Parker

1816 N. Clark St. • 312-254-4747 • www.jparkerchicago.com

Seeing the city from a rooftop is a quintessential Chicago experience for locals and vacationers alike. The J. Parker, situated on top of **Hotel Lincoln**, has some of the best unobstructed views of **North Avenue Beach**, **Lincoln Park**, and **Lake Michigan**. Enjoy the fire pits, a colorful mural, live music, and the minimalist decor. Order small- or large-plate menu items or visit for the breakfast buffet. If you're concerned about the potential for inclement weather, don't worry; the outdoor atrium space is enclosed by a fully retractable glass roof.

While the J. Parker is a family-friendly space before late evening, another option if you have your kids in tow is to visit the rooftop, snap photos of the view, and then dine in one of the hotel's other restaurants—**Sushi Suite 202**, an intimate speakeasy of sorts; the **Kennison**, with delicious American fare; or **Sushi by Bou**, an upscale, timed experience.

The J. Parker (Courtesy of The J. Parker)

Nearby Alternatives

Play: Oz Park

Young and young-at-heart love visiting the whimsical Oz Park, a 14-acre green space in the heart of Lincoln Park. See the Tin Man, the Cowardly Lion, the Scarecrow, and Dorothy with Toto sculptures. Explore the flower-filled "Emerald Garden" and "Dorothy's Playlot," with climb-on structures, swings, and slides, donated by Dorothy Melamerson, a local retired schoolteacher.

2021 N. Burling St.
312-742-7898
www.chicagoparkdistrict.com

Discover: Chicago History Museum

The family-friendly Chicago History Museum takes you across a timeline from the Great Chicago Fire to the present day. Permanent exhibits: City on Fire: Chicago 1871, Chicago: Crossroads of America, Facing Freedom in America, Sensing Chicago, the Great Chicago Adventure Film, the Fifth Star Challenge, and Lincoln's Chicago.

1601 N. Clark St.
312-642-4600
www.chicagohistory.org

Play: North Avenue Beach

You'll spot the popular North Avenue Beach, with its ocean liner–inspired beach house, right away. Located east of the zoo, it offers not only stellar skyline views but also an abundance of conveniences provided by **Castaways Bar and Grill**, **Shore Club**, **Lakeshore Bike 'n Tune**, **Chicago SUP**, **Kayak Chicago**, and **Jet Ski Chicago**.

1601 N. Jean-Baptiste Pointe DuSable Lake Shore Dr.
312-74-BEACH
www.chicagoparkdistrict.com

Discover: Kingston Mines

Within walking distance of the **DePaul University Art Museum**, **Wiggly Field Dog Park**, the **Wiener's Circle**, and the **Neighborhood Hotel** is one of the oldest continually operating blues clubs in Chicago: Kingston Mines (1968). Eat Southern-fried okra, barbecue, catfish, red beans and rice, or corn bread while you listen to a show.

2548 N. Halsted
773-477-4646
www.kingstonmines.com

Trip Planning

Lincoln Park Chamber of Commerce

2468 N. Lincoln Ave.
773-880-5200
www.lincolnparkchamber.com

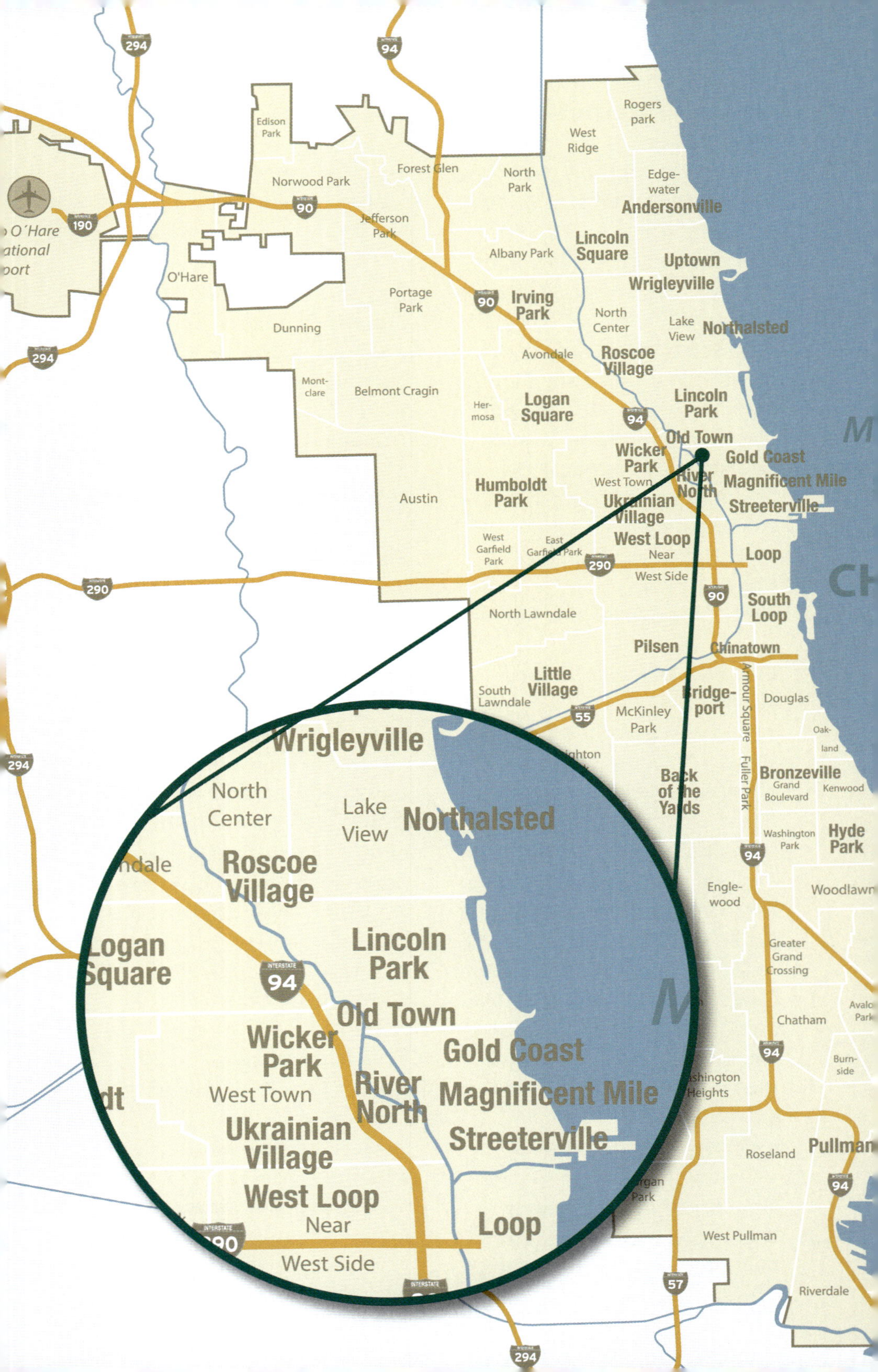
Edison Park
Norwood Park
Forest Glen
North Park
West Ridge
Rogers park
Edge-water
Andersonville
Jefferson Park
O'Hare
Albany Park
Lincoln Square
Uptown
Wrigleyville
Portage Park
Irving Park
North Center
Lake View
Northalsted
Dunning
Avondale
Roscoe Village
Mont-clare
Belmont Cragin
Her-mosa
Logan Square
Lincoln Park
Old Town
Gold Coast
Wicker Park
West Town
River North
Magnificent Mile
Austin
Humboldt Park
Ukrainian Village
Streeterville
West Garfield Park
East Garfield Park
West Loop
Near West Side
Loop
South Loop
North Lawndale
Pilsen
Chinatown
South Lawndale
Little Village
Bridge-port
McKinley Park
Douglas
Armour Square
Fuller Park
Oak-land
Back of the Yards
Bronzeville
Grand Boulevard
Kenwood
Washington Park
Hyde Park
Engle-wood
Woodlawn
Greater Grand Crossing
Chatham
Burn-side
Roseland
Pullman
West Pullman
Riverdale
294
94
190
90
290
55
57

OLD TOWN

WITH VICTORIAN-ERA EDIFICES and historic churches—including St. Michael's, one of the seven buildings to survive the Great Chicago Fire—Old Town and Old Town Triangle are worth exploring. Stroll the tree-lined streets full of coffee shops, boutiques, restaurants, and entertainment options like the Second City and the Steppenwolf Theater Company. Lake Michigan and North Avenue Beach are nearby. The sense of community is strong in this Near North Side area, settled by German immigrants in 1850.

Whether you're spending a day or an entire weekend here, you can't go wrong mixing and matching the following top venues.

The boundaries are often disputed depending on who you ask, but a smart place to start is on Wells Street, between the Old Town gates, with North Avenue at one end and Division Street at the other. You'll find plenty of eateries and bars here, including the VIG, 80 Proof, Old Town Ale House (a pet haunt of Anthony Bourdain and Roger Ebert), Old Town Pour House, Uproar Chicago, and Twin Anchors (frequented by Frank Sinatra). Old Town is the nexus between the Gold Coast, Lincoln Park, and River North—three of Chicago's most popular neighborhoods.

The Second City

1616 N. Wells St., 2nd Floor • 312-337-3992 • www.secondcity.com

Old Town is home to one of the world's most famous comedy clubs, The Second City, showcasing nightly entertainment. Known as the birthplace of modern American improv, many prominent comedians and *Saturday Night Live* stars got their start here, including Bill Murray, Gilda Radner, John Candy, Dan Aykroyd, Eugene Levy, Catherine O'Hara, Chris Farley, John and Jim Belushi, Martin Short, Steve Carell, Tina Fey, Amy Poehler, Stephen Colbert, Aidy Bryant, and, well, you get the idea. What began as a comedy cabaret in 1959 has grown to include not only theaters and training centers in Chicago, Toronto, and Hollywood, but also a range of TV, film, and digital productions.

Along with several shows on multiple stages—Chicago Mainstage, e.t.c. Theater, and Up Comedy Club—the Second City is notorious for its Second City Training Center. Adults and kids can take comedy and acting classes, join camps, and participate in writing programs to hone their skills.

The Second City (Courtesy of Wendy Altschuler)

Courtesy of Wendy Altschuler

A Red Orchid Theater

1531 N. Wells St. • 312-943-8722 • www.aredorchidtheater.org

✔ Chicago is very much a theater town, and seeing a live show is an essential experience when visiting. An ensemble of artists present plays from all over the globe at the award-winning A Red Orchid Theater, founded in 1993 by Guy Van Swearingen, Michael Shannon (*Groundhog Day*, *8 Mile*, *The Shape of Water*), and Lawrence Grimm. Watch an intimate production in the 70-seat storefront theater space, with detailed sets and up-close action—you'll be fully absorbed into the scenes. Imaginative writers, directors, and performers come together to produce magic at a venue where stage productions written by local Chicago playwrights are the theater's specialty.

Eat dinner at one of the preferred partners for perks: **Kamehachi** for sushi, located in the same building; **Adobo Grill** for Mexican favorites; the **Kennison**, situated at **Hotel Lincoln**, for new American fare; **Orso's**, a family owned and operated restaurant for Italian; or **80 Proof**, which has loads of vegan options.

Topo Gigio Ristoranté

1516 N. Wells St. • 312-266-9355 • www.topogigiochicago.com

If you're visiting the city during well-loved events and festivals like the **Old Town Art Fair**, the **Wells Street Art Festival**, or the **Chicago Air and Water Show**, you'll have plenty of great street food options from Old Town restaurants as well as other Chicago classics at your fingertips. Outside of open-air grab-and-go noshes, which are fun when exploring the dining scene on foot, you might want to enjoy a proper sit-down meal at one of the best Tuscan-style Italian restaurants in the city.

The award-winning Topo Gigio has a large menu with plenty of possibilities—even the pickiest of eaters in your family will find something they adore here. Dine on the outdoor patio, complete with string lights and heat lamps (if it's chilly), or the charming front terrace, with flower boxes and great people watching. Both are ideal spots to relax and appreciate your meal, especially with little ones in tow.

Topo Gigio Ristoranté (Courtesy of Wendy Altschuler)

Nearby Alternatives

Discover: Germania Club

See the Germania Club, a red brick building where moving newfangled art exhibits like Immersive Van Gogh and Frida: Immersive Dream have been held through **Lighthouse ArtSpace**. Built in 1889 and featuring ornamental detail, this historic landmark was once a social outlet for Chicago immigrants and the original home of a German American singing society.

108 W. Germania Pl.
844-307-4644
www.vangoghchicago.com

Shop: The Fudge Pot

The Fudge Pot is not only an Old Town staple but a Chicago institution. Sweets have been made onsite since 1963. Over 1,000 different chocolate shapes are created in this small shop, including a Statue of Liberty bust, Eiffel tower, Oscar trophy, hot dogs, and more.

1532 N. Wells St.
312-943-1777
www.thefudgepotchicago.com

Play: Zanies Comedy Club

While the **Second City** is known for improv, nearby Zanies Comedy Club is popular for stand-up, featuring national headliners every night. Zanies has been making folks laugh since 1978; notable past performers include Jay Leno, Jerry Seinfeld, Kathy Griffin, Kevin Hart, Hannibal Buress, Jimmy Fallon, Sarah Silverman, Aziz Ansari, and Chris Rock.

1548 N. Wells St.
312-337-4027
www.chicago.zanies.com

Shop: The Spice House

Whether you're a foodie, chef, or someone who wants to tickle their olfactory sense, a visit to the Spice House is for you. Founded in 1957, with another shop in Evanston, the Spice House offers a myriad of global spices, herbs, extracts, and blends. Next, pop into nearby **Old Town Oil**.

1512 N. Wells St.
312-274-0378
www.thespicehouse.com

Trip Planning

Old Town Merchants & Residents Association

1543 N. Wells St.
312-951-6106
www.oldtownchicago.org

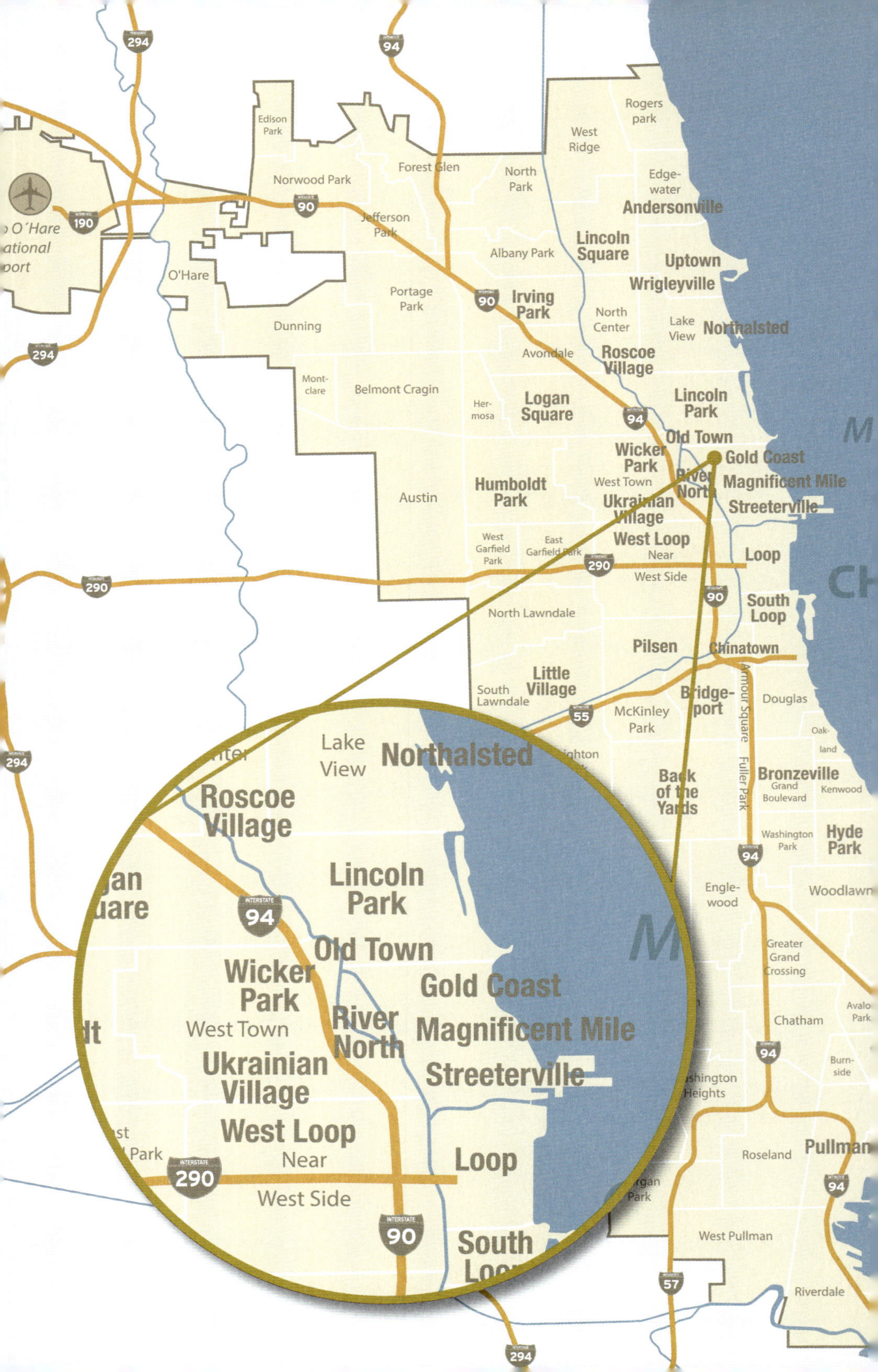
294
94
Edison Park
Rogers park
West Ridge
Edgewater
Norwood Park
Forest Glen
North Park
Andersonville
190
90
Jefferson Park
Lincoln Square
Albany Park
Uptown
O'Hare
Wrigleyville
Portage Park
Irving Park
North Center
Lake View
Northalsted
Dunning
Avondale
Roscoe Village
Montclare
Belmont Cragin
Hermosa
Logan Square
Lincoln Park
Old Town
Wicker Park
Gold Coast
West Town
River North
Magnificent Mile
Humboldt Park
Austin
Ukrainian Village
Streeterville
West Garfield Park
East Garfield Park
West Loop
Near West Side
Loop
290
South Loop
North Lawndale
Pilsen
Chinatown
Little Village
South Lawndale
55
McKinley Park
Bridgeport
Armour Square
Douglas
Oakland
Fuller Park
Back of the Yards
Bronzeville
Grand Boulevard
Kenwood
Washington Park
Hyde Park
Englewood
Woodlawn
Greater Grand Crossing
Chatham
Avalon Park
Burnside
Washington Heights
Roseland
Pullman
West Pullman
Riverdale
57

GOLD COAST

ONE OF CHICAGO'S wealthiest sons, Potter Palmer, built his mansion along the lakefront just north of downtown in the late 1800s, and it wasn't long until others followed suit. Part of the city's Near North Side community area, the Gold Coast, listed on the National Register of Historic Places, is one of the most well-heeled neighborhoods of Chicago.

Beyond swanky residences and hotels, including Hugh Hefner's original Playboy Mansion (now luxury condos), locals and tourists love visiting the beach on the shores of Lake Michigan, looking for something fresh to wear in the Windy City's premiere shopping districts, and dining at award-winning restaurants. If you have kids in tow, bring them to one of the cupcake shops—Sprinkles Chicago has an actual cupcake ATM—and stay at the Four Seasons Hotel Chicago where kids can swim, get an in-room ice cream cart delivery, and play at the Kids Club. Wondering how to spend the day in one of the most pedestrian-friendly neighborhoods? Bring your wallet and your sense of adventure and keep reading.

International Museum of Surgical Science

1524 N. Lake Shore Dr. • 312-642-6502 • www.imss.org

On the north end of the Gold Coast, near the lakefront, sits one of the most underrated museums in Chicago. North America's only museum devoted to surgery, the International Museum of Surgical Science is a surprise in more ways than one. Not only will you see art and artifacts spanning the history of medicine, but you'll also learn things you would never have known otherwise. Wander this early 20th-century mansion's four floors and explore the **Hall of Murals**, **Hall of Immortals**, **Apothecary**, **Nursing Gallery**, and **Pain Gallery**. See an amputation saw with reversible blade from the 1500s; original X-rays taken in 1910 by Emil Grubbe, a radiology pioneer; the Lindbergh perfusion pump, invented by the famous aviator Charles Lindbergh and Nobel Prize–winning surgeon Alexis Carrel; and skulls from ancient Peru. You'll also see over 600 wondrous prints, paintings, and sculptures, including a plaster cast made from the death mask of Napoleon in 1821.

International Museum of Surgical Science
(Courtesy of Michael Robinson, International Museum of Surgical Science)

Courtesy of Wendy Altschuler

Oak Street Beach

100 North Lake Shore Dr. • 312-74-BEACH • www.chicagoparkdistrict.com

✓ Beyond the opulent buildings and stunning architecture, the Gold Coast is prized for its, well, coast. Carve out plenty of time to explore the famous Lakefront Trail and Oak Street Beach. Most folks know that Chicago is the birthplace of the skyscraper, and one of the best spots to snap photographs of the skyline is at this beach. This is your gateway to swimming, biking, rollerblading, volleyball, and relaxing in the sun; amenities here include bike, volleyball, and chair rentals. Food and beverages are available at **Whispers at Oak Street Beach**. Popular amateur and professional volleyball tournaments also take place here each summer.

Be sure to see the 260-foot-long Jeff Zimmermann mural, "You Know What You Should Do," located at the access point to the Oak Street Beach underpass. The mural is a reminder to keep the beach and lake clean by avoiding littering and feeding wildlife.

The Drake

140 E. Walton Pl.
312-787-2200 • www.thedrakehotel.com

☑ An iconic hotel, the Drake, part of Historic Hotels of America and listed in the National Register of Historic Places, was a staple in the Roaring Twenties and beyond. Famous patrons include Bing Crosby, Walt Disney, George Gershwin, and Charles Lindbergh. Marilyn Monroe and Joe Dimaggio carved their initials into the wooden bar. This Beaux-Arts hotel is a flashy, must-see locale.

For dining and Prohibition-era cocktails, call on **Coq d'Or**, Chicago's second establishment to receive a liquor license. The **Fountain Court**, now called the **Palm Court**, has been the most admired place to enjoy tea and noshes in all the city (even Queen Elizabeth II of England and Princess Diana have visited). Choose from 17 different tea blends, served in individual pots, and fill your belly with mini sandwiches, scones, and treats, presented on three-tiered trays. Parents will love bringing their kids to the Prince & Princess Afternoon Tea service.

The Drake
(Courtesy of Wendy Altschuler)

Nearby Alternatives

Shop: Oak Street District

It's not named the Gold Coast for nothing. High-end shopping abounds, especially in the area around Oak Street. Showrooms and boutiques—**Armani**, **Prada**, **Chanel**, **Dolce & Gabbana**, **Louboutin**, **Hermes**—are nestled along the tree-lined street, making you feel like you've discovered a secret pocket of the city.

E. Oak St. and N. Michigan Ave.

Eat: Lou Malnati's

You can't visit Chicago without trying out some of our famous deep-dish pizza. Arguably the best, Lou Malnati's is known for its flaky, buttery crust, layered with slices of Wisconsin mozzarella cheese, and topped with chunky tomato sauce. Balance out the affluent Gold Coast experience with an affordable and yummy pie.

1120 N. State St.
312-725-7777
www.loumalnatis.com

Discover: Newberry Library

Home to 1.6 million books, 600,000 maps, and 5 million manuscript pages, the Newberry Library, founded in 1887, is quite the local gem. Learn about human history as you wander through the hallowed halls, reading rooms, and exhibition galleries or take part in one of the humanities programs.

60 W. Walton St.
312-943-9090
www.newberry.org

Play: Washington Square Park

Across from the **Newberry Library** sits a small and lovely park, featuring a floral garden and large fountain. In the spring and summer, you may see a wedding ceremony in progress, as Washington Square Park is picturesque and well located near popular hotels like **Waldorf Astoria Chicago** and **Sofitel Chicago**.

901 N. Clark St.
312-742-7895
www.palmspringsairmuseum.org

Trip Planning

Chicago History Museum

Gold Coast Walking Tour
www.chicagohistory.org/gold-coast-walking-tour

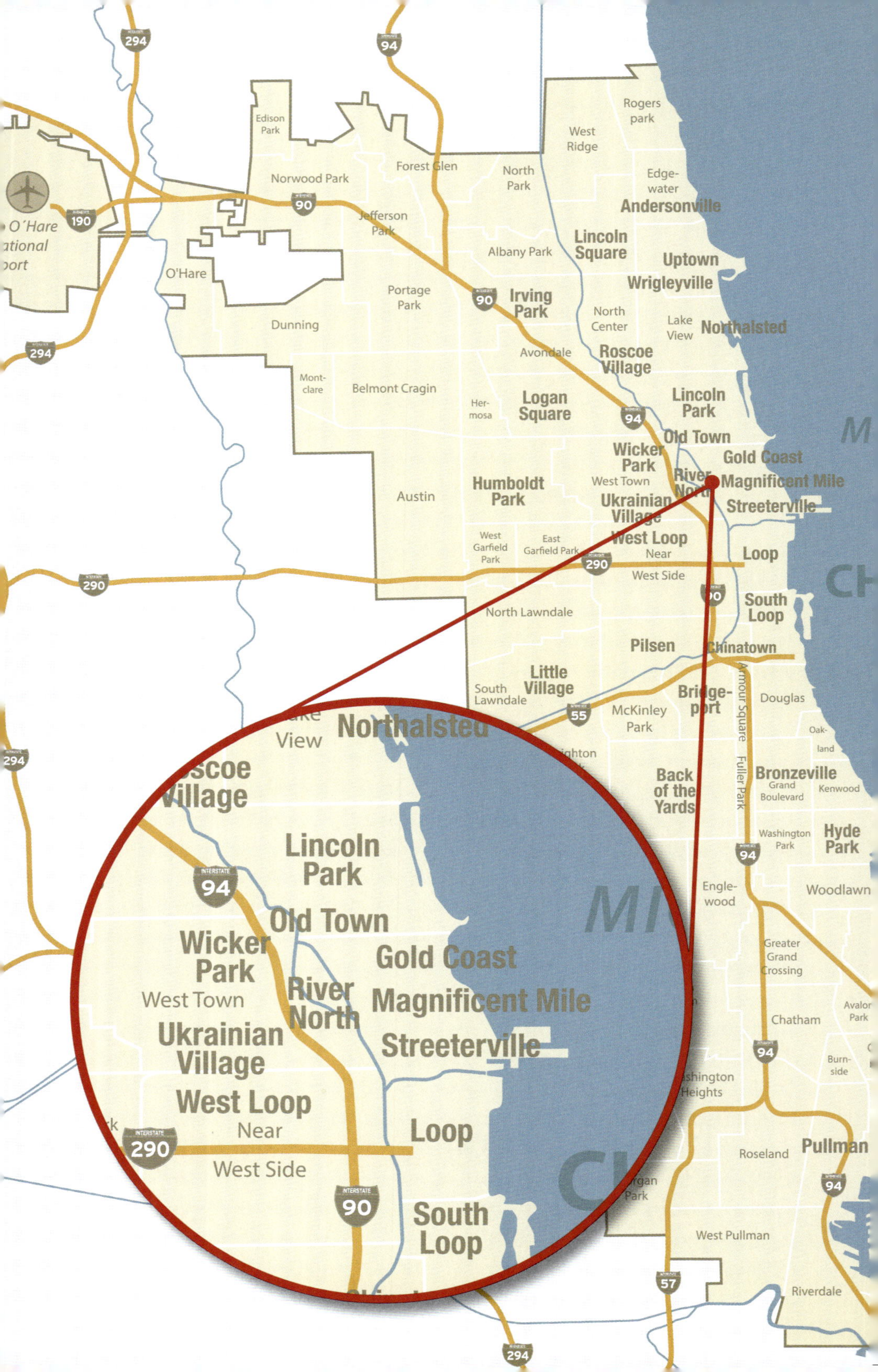

Edison Park
Norwood Park
Forest Glen
North Park
West Ridge
Rogers park
Edge-water
Andersonville
Lincoln Square
Uptown
Wrigleyville
Albany Park
Jefferson Park
O'Hare International Airport
O'Hare
Portage Park
Irving Park
North Center
Lake View
Northalsted
Dunning
Avondale
Roscoe Village
Mont-clare
Belmont Cragin
Her-mosa
Logan Square
Lincoln Park
Old Town
Wicker Park
Gold Coast
River North
Magnificent Mile
West Town
Humboldt Park
Austin
Ukrainian Village
Streeterville
West Garfield Park
East Garfield Park
West Loop
Near West Side
Loop
North Lawndale
South Loop
Pilsen
Chinatown
Little Village
South Lawndale
McKinley Park
Bridge-port
Armour Square
Douglas
Oak-land
Back of the Yards
Fuller Park
Bronzeville
Grand Boulevard
Kenwood
Washington Park
Hyde Park
Engle-wood
Woodlawn
Greater Grand Crossing
Chatham
Avalon Park
Burn-side
Washington Heights
Roseland
Pullman
Morgan Park
West Pullman
Riverdale

MAGNIFICENT MILE

THE MAGNIFICENT MILE is one of the city's top avenues to explore. From Randolph Street to the south, North Avenue to the north, Lake Michigan to the east, and the Chicago River to the west, this district, in addition to the 13-block stretch on North Michigan Avenue, kisses five popular Chicago neighborhoods: New Eastside, Streeterville, Gold Coast, Old Town, and River North. Beyond trendy restaurants, shopping, and landmark architecture, you'll find some of the Windy City's best hotels.

Begin your adventure at DuSable Bridge, a historic two-level bascule bridge, once called Michigan Avenue Bridge, constructed in the early 1900s. Travel north, past the Wrigley Building, completed in 1924, and the Tribune Tower, finished in 1925—see stones from famous sites around the world like the Great Wall of China, the Taj Mahal, and the Cathedral of Notre Dame embedded in the facade. Make your way to the Chicago Water Tower, one of the few buildings to survive the Great Chicago Fire of 1871. Finish the day on the 94th floor of the Hancock.

Museum of Ice Cream

435 N. Michigan Ave. • www.museumoficecream.com

✓ The newly opened Museum of Ice Cream, located in the historic Chicago Tribune building on Michigan Avenue, is a unique experience that is fun for the whole family. You'll want to add this Willy Wonka-like escapade to your Magnificent Mile itinerary. (Other locations include New York City, Austin, and Singapore.) Learn about the history of ice cream through 14 interactive installations at this dessert-themed, multi-hued carnival of sorts. Ride the imaginative pink Sprink-L line (a nod to our public transportation system), plop in the sprinkle-filled pool, and check out the golf on the putt-putt course. Kids will adore the cookie carousel, the fun house mirror maze, and the balloon room. Adults will dig the inventive craft cocktails. Five free-flow dessert stations, including Chicago fan favorites like ice cream hot dogs and shaved iced, delight all visitors. In truth, this is an Instagram-worthy destination—you'll love taking photographs as you wander around the museum.

Museum of Ice Cream (Courtesy of Will Ellis)

John Hancock Center (Courtesy of Wendy Altschuler)

John Hancock Center

875 N. Michigan Ave. • 888-875-8439 • www.360chicago.com

Even though the name changed to 875 North Michigan Avenue in 2018, this building, built by Skidmore, Owings & Merrill, will always be known to locals as the **John Hancock Center**. This 100-story skyscraper, once the second-tallest building in the world after the Empire State Building, is home to **360 CHICAGO**.

Visit the 94th floor's observation deck for some of the finest views of the city and Lake Michigan, 1,000 feet above the Magnificent Mile. Adventure seekers will love **TILT**, Chicago's highest thrill ride with downward facing views. Visit the bar and café, **Bar 94**, for light bites and local brews. Or make dinner reservations at the **Signature Room** at the 95th and enjoy a cocktail at the **Signature Lounge** at the 96th—perfect for viewing the sunset! Make sure you snap photos of this iconic building, recognizable for its tapered design, complete with massive X-bracing on the exterior.

Billy Goat Tavern

430 N. Michigan Ave., Lower Level • 312-222-1525 • www.billygoattavern.com

✔ At the original Billy Goat Tavern, a favorite rooted in local lore, you'll find yourself chanting the phrase made popular by Greek immigrant and owner William "Billy Goat" Sianis, and preserved by *Saturday Night Live*'s John Belushi, Dan Aykroyd, and Bill Murray: "Cheezborger, cheezborger, cheezborger. No Pepsi . . . Coke." Sianis bought the **Lincoln Tavern**, located across from **Chicago Stadium**, in 1934, and when a goat wandered inside after falling off a truck, he adopted it and changed the name of the bar to Billy Goat Tavern. In 1945, Sianis tried to bring his goat to **Wrigley Field** during the Chicago Cubs World Series, and when he was denied entry, he put a curse on the Cubs.

The tavern moved in 1964 to its present location and expanded to other areas of the city. Order a Cheezborger, stacked with pickles, double cheese, and no lettuce or tomatoes.

Billy Goat Tavern (Courtesy of Billy Goat Tavern)

Nearby Alternatives

Shop: Water Tower Place

With a buzzy dining scene and a legendary shopping district, Chicago's Magnificent Mile offers numerous shopping opportunities, including **900 North Michigan Shops**, the **Shops at North Bridge**, and avenue boutiques. Find **American Girl**, **Chicago Sports Museum**, **Broadway Playhouse**, **Ritz-Carlton Chicago**, **Wao Bao**, and **Garrett Popcorn** at Water Tower Place.

835 N. Michigan Ave.
312-440-3165
www.shopwatertower.com

Discover: The Richard H. Driehaus Museum

Venture back to the Gilded Age with a visit to the Richard H. Driehaus Museum, a decorative arts feast for the senses set inside a 19th-century mansion known as the Marble Palace. Enjoy art, fashion, and design exhibits; marvel at the stained-glass dome; and learn at civic programs in the ballroom.

40 E. Erie St.
312-482-8933
www.driehausmuseum.org

Play: Candy Crawl

Not only can you see plenty of architecture in the birthplace of the skyscraper, but you can also eat your weight in candy. From **Teuscher Chocolates of Switzerland** to **Ghirardelli Ice Cream & Chocolate Shop** to **Fannie May**, there's plenty to choose from. Start your candy crawl at **It'Sugar**.

717 N. Michigan Ave.
410-379-2794
www.itsugar.com

Discover: Intercontinental Chicago Magnificent Mile

More than 70 hotels are on or near the Mag Mile, including **Four Seasons Hotel Chicago**, **Omni Chicago Hotel**, and the **Peninsula Chicago**. The InterContinental Chicago Magnificent Mile (1929) is a paragon of opulence with its Prohibition-era pool, chandelier-clad ballrooms, and hand-painted murals. Dine on-site at **Michael Jordan's Steak House**.

505 N. Michigan Ave.
312-944-4100
www.icchicagohotel.com

Trip Planning

The Magnificent Mile Association

625 N. Michigan Ave.
312-642-3570
www.themagnificentmile.com

Rogers park
West Ridge
Edison Park
Norwood Park
Forest Glen
North Park
Edge-water
Andersonville
Lincoln Square
Uptown
Wrigleyville
Jefferson Park
Albany Park
O'Hare
Portage Park
Irving Park
North Center
Lake View
Northalsted
Dunning
Avondale
Roscoe Village
Mont-clare
Belmont Cragin
Her-mosa
Logan Square
Lincoln Park
Old Town
Wicker Park
Gold Coast
Humboldt Park
West Town
River North
Magnificent Mile
Austin
Ukrainian Village
Streeterville
West Garfield Park
East Garfield Park
West Loop
Near West Side
Loop
South Loop
North Lawndale
Pilsen
Chinatown
South Lawndale
Little Village
McKinley Park
Bridge-port
Armour Square
Douglas
Oak-land
Back of the Yards
Fuller Park
Bronzeville
Grand Boulevard
Kenwood
Washington Park
Hyde Park
Engle-wood
Woodlawn
Greater Grand Crossing
Avalon Park
Chatham
Burn-side
Washington Heights
Roseland
Pullman
West Pullman
Riverdale
294
94
90
190
290
55
57

RIVER NORTH

LOCATED ON CHICAGO'S affluent Near North Side, directly north of the river, River North is an area of the city that was once a major transportation hub, dominated by factories and warehouses. (theMART still has railroad tracks underneath the building.) In the 1970s, the River North Gallery District, the largest concentration of art galleries in America outside of Manhattan, developed.

Now the area is home to popular restaurants, nightlife, and entertainment venues as well as a design district with showrooms and shops full of home furnishings. You'll see plenty of historic towers and buildings like the Wrigley Building, Holy Name Cathedral, Marina City, Merchandise Mart, 330 N. Wabash (AMA Plaza, IBM Building), and House of Blues. The Godfrey Hotel Chicago, Moxy Chicago Downtown, Aloft Chicago Downtown River North, 21c Museum Hotel Chicago, the Peninsula Chicago, the Gwen, and the Langham Chicago are all nearby and offer something unique for visitors. Whether you love art and design, architecture, good food, or adventures along the riverfront, a visit here is a must.

theMART

222 W. Merchandise Mart Plz. • 312-527-7600 • www.themart.com

✔ Massive and imposing, theMART, formerly known as the Merchandise Mart, was the largest building in the world when it opened in 1930. Just imagine what over four million square feet of floor space looked like back then. Situated at the junction of the Chicago River's branches, this Art Deco building was built by Marshall Field & Co. and was later owned by the Kennedy family for over half a century. One of the world's leading commercial buildings and wholesale design centers, theMART stretches over two city blocks and stands 25 stories tall.

In addition to hundreds of showrooms featuring custom home furnishings and interior design, several open-to-the-public shows and events happen each year, including **LuxeHome Chill** and **One of a Kind Holiday Show**. **Art on theMART** is the world's largest video projection art installation, where you can marvel at multi-hued nightly projections on the building's facade. Nearby fun: **AceBounce**, **Doughnut Vault**, and **Raised Urban Rooftop Bar**.

theMART (Courtesy of Wendy Altschuler)

House of Blues (Courtesy of Wendy Altschuler)

House of Blues

329 N. Dearborn St. • 312-923-2000 • www.houseofblues.com/chicago

✔ Part of Bertrand Goldberg's Marina City, the House of Blues sits inside an eye-catching, saddle-shaped building by the Chicago River. The interior, modeled after the Estavovski Opera House in Prague, is just as stunning.

Founded by Isaac Tigrett, a co-founder of Hard Rock Café, and Dan Aykroyd, a star in the film *The Blues Brothers*, House of Blues joined the Live Nation network in 2006. Even though the House of Blues is an American chain of concert halls and restaurants offering a variety of shows for guests of all ages, seeing a live concert here is a classic Chicago experience. Hear folk, country, hip-hop, rap, soul, rock, pop, electronic, jazz, or blues music. Participate in a dance party. The family-friendly Gospel Brunch, held on Sundays, is an all-you-can-eat breakfast buffet featuring flavorful, Southern-inspired fare. The singing, dancing, and music are sure to give your arms goosebumps and elevate your mood.

Travelle at the Langham

330 N. Wabash Ave., 2nd Floor • 312-923-7705 • www.travellechicago.com

✓ Many Chicagoans will tell you that in River North if you want steak, go to **Bavette's Bar** and **Boeuf**; for ramen, **Ramen-san**; Mexican, **Tzuco**; Peruvian, **Tanta**; French, **Brindille**; seafood, **GT Fish & Oyster**; Italian, **Eataly**; and Mediterranean, **Ema**.

But, for elevated American fare, open for breakfast through dinner, make reservations at Travelle at the Langham, located along the Chicago River on the second floor of a skyscraper designed by Ludwig Mies van der Rohe. Travelle, a play on the word *travel*, is perfect for out-of-towners and well-heeled locals. For a special night, arrange for the Chef's Table, where you'll be privy to the kitchen for an interactive dining experience. Wine aficionados will love the Cellar Table, a semi-private space in full view of an extensive wine collection. The mid-century modern lounge offers stunning views of the Chicago River and cityscape and is ideal for mingling before dinner.

Travelle at the Langham (Courtesy of Wendy Altschuler)

Nearby Alternatives

Discover: Museum of Broadcast Communications

From television and radio memorabilia to a working studio to plaques of National Radio Hall of Fame inductees to Oprah's Door, this museum is fun for all. Afterward, visit **Harry Caray's Italian Steakhouse** next door and gawk at the Chicago sports memorabilia and photographs of famous diners.

360 N. State St.
312-245-8200
www.museum.tv

Play: Chicago Electric Boat Company

Surprise the family and rent a boat from the Chicago Electric Boat Company. You'll tour the Chicago River at your own pace, beginning at either **Marina City** or **Chicago Riverwalk/City Winery**. Choose the appropriate boat size for your group and don your captain's hat, or, if you prefer, hire a guide for the outing.

300 N. State St. or
11 W. Riverwalk S.
312-644-6411
www.chicagoelectricboats.com

Discover: The Comedy Bar

With a performance stage and outdoor rooftop terrace, as well as access to Chicago's famous cheesy deep-dish pizza from **Gino's East**, the Comedy Bar is perfect for a casual date night or a friends' night out. Prepare to laugh during a live stand-up comedy show, and wear your stretchy pants.

162 E. Superior St.
312-836-0499
www.comedybar.com/chicago

Play: Wateriders and Chicago Riverwalk

Launching from the East Bank Club, go on a kayaking adventure with Wateriders, the first kayaking tour offered on the Chicago River: Choose from among the History and Architecture Tour, the Sunset Paddle, the Navy Pier Fireworks Paddle, the Ghosts and Gangsters Tour, or the Moonlight Paddle. Afterward, explore the Chicago Riverwalk, one of the best outdoor spaces in the city.

500 N. Kingsbury St.
312-953-9287
www.wateriders.com

Trip Planning

Choose Chicago

301 E. Cermak Rd.
312-567-8500
www.choosechicago.com

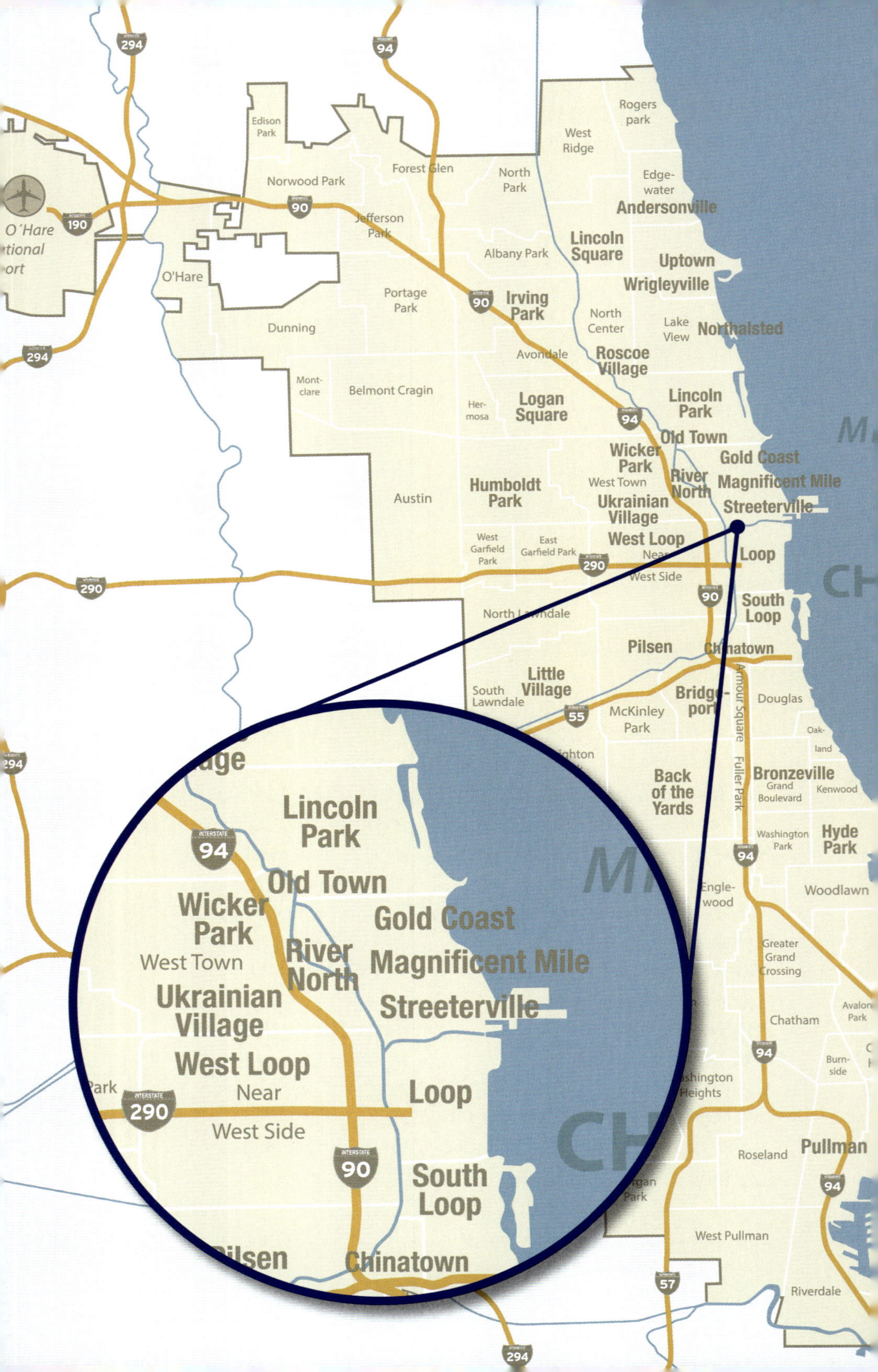

294
94
Edison Park
Rogers park
West Ridge
Edge-water
Andersonville
Norwood Park
Forest Glen
North Park
190
90
Jefferson Park
Lincoln Square
Albany Park
Uptown
O'Hare
Wrigleyville
Portage Park
Irving Park
North Center
Lake View
Northalsted
Dunning
Avondale
Roscoe Village
Mont-clare
Belmont Cragin
Her-mosa
Logan Square
Lincoln Park
Old Town
Wicker Park
Gold Coast
River North
Magnificent Mile
West Town
Humboldt Park
Austin
Ukrainian Village
Streeterville
West Garfield Park
East Garfield Park
West Loop
Loop
290
Near West Side
South Loop
North Lawndale
Pilsen
Chinatown
Little Village
South Lawndale
Bridgeport
Douglas
Armour Square
55
McKinley Park
Oak-land
Back of the Yards
Fuller Park
Bronzeville
Grand Boulevard
Kenwood
Washington Park
Hyde Park
Engle-wood
Woodlawn
Greater Grand Crossing
Chatham
Avalon Park
Burn-side
Washington Heights
Roseland
Pullman
Morgan Park
West Pullman
57
Riverdale
Near
West Side

STREETERVILLE

STREETERVILLE IS A well-visited neighborhood in the Near North Side community area, just north of the Chicago River. Fun fact: most of the land here is reclaimed sand bar. Named after the infamous George Wellington "Cap" Streeter, a real estate trickster who tried to defraud wealthy landowners in the late 1880s, Streeterville is near the Magnificent Mile and Lake Michigan. It's home to Navy Pier, one of the Windy City's top attractions; you'll have easy access to family-friendly fun like amusement rides, gift shops, and good eats. Plan on experiencing Chicago via the water on a dinner boat cruise or speedboat ride. Kids will love the children's museum, nighttime fireworks, and multi-age events and programs.

Beyond the pier, which nearly nine million people visit annually, marvel at skyscrapers, museums, and theaters. The Museum of Contemporary Art is a must-see. Ohio Street Beach is picture-perfect for swimming and wiggling your toes in the sand, and the Lakefront Trail, where you can run, stroll, or ride bicycles, is a great way to enjoy the outdoors.

Museum of Contemporary Art

220 E. Chicago Ave. • 312-280-2660 • www.mcachicago.org

☑ One of the coolest museums in the city is the Museum of Contemporary Art, planted east of the **Chicago Water Tower**, **Lookingglass Theatre Company**, and **Seneca Park**. With a collection that includes more than 2,000 pieces of art from local and international exhibits, there's much to see, including in the **Atrium**, the **Commons**, the **Sculpture Garden**, the **Street**, and the **Marisol** restaurant. The museum offers programs where you can listen to live music, watch dance performances, interact with artists, learn at a special talk, or watch a screening. Workshops and youth-led events are a fun way to study sculpture, web design, nature drawing, literary art, screen printing, and a myriad of other immersive arts. One of the largest museums in the world dedicated to contemporary art, this institution has been showcasing works created by living artists since 1967. Don't miss the gift shop—it's one of the best in the city!

Museum of Contemporary Art (Courtesy of Wendy Altschuler)

Chicago Children's Museum (Courtesy of Ranvestel Photographic, Choose Chicago)

☑ Chicago Children's Museum

700 E. Grand Ave., Ste. 127 • 312-527-1000
www.chicagochildrensmuseum.org

There's always something joyful going on at the Chicago Children's Museum, full of rotating and permanent exhibits and programs that are ideal for kids of all ages. The littlest ones in your group will love the **Treehouse Trails**, **Kids Town**, and **Pritzker Playspace**. Older children can climb through tunnels in **Cloud Buster**, captain their own ship at the **Boats** exhibit, dig for bones at **Dinosaur Expedition**, design skyscrapers at **Skyline**, create in the **Art Studio**, and use real tools to build unique inventions in the **Tinkering Lab**. Learn about fire safety at the **Play It Safe** exhibit, shop in a grocery store, work on a car, and drive a CTA bus during your time at this museum. The role-playing youngsters experience while interacting with other children teaches them how to problem solve while having fun at the same time.

Lirica

900 E. Grand Ave. • 872-710-5700
www.liricarestaurant.com

✓ **Navy Pier**, originally designed for shipping and recreational purposes, opened to the public in 1916. New to the pier, piloting in an era of hospitality, is the first and only hotel, the nautical-themed **Sable** at Navy Pier, a Curio Collection by Hilton. Every guest room enjoys lake and skyline views from floor-to-ceiling windows.

Arguably, the best restaurant on Navy Pier is Lirica, virtuosos in Latin and Iberian-inspired cuisine. It's open all day, breakfast through dinner, and you can order small or big plates, handhelds, or salads. A special menu is designed just for kids, and vegetarian and gluten-free options are available. The prix-fixe menu is perfect for sharing with friends and family and for tasting chef specialties. Not to be missed are the curated cocktails. Try the Oaxacan Old Fashioned, Old Cuban, Frozen Sangria, or Passionfruit Vanilla Mojito. After dinner, visit **Offshore**, the world's largest rooftop bar. The views from this 20,000-square-foot terrace are incredible.

Navy Pier, Home of Lirica (Courtesy of Choose Chicago)

Nearby Alternatives

Play: Ohio Street Beach

Tucked north of **Jane Addams Memorial Park**, Ohio Street Beach is the best in the city for open-water swimming. With access to the Lakefront Trail, families and friends can spend the day here enjoying skyline views and outdoor activities. For noshes, pop into beachfront **Café Oliva**, situated in Olive Park.

600 N. Lake Shore Dr.
312-74-BEACH
www.chicagoparkdistrict.com

Discover: Navy Pier Beer Garden

First, order a Snow Cream from **Snow Dragon Shavery** or an original Chicago-style popcorn from **Garrett Popcorn Shops**, then head to Navy Pier Beer Garden, where from May to October you can listen to outdoor music for free. The garden is also the best spot to view the summer and New Year's Eve fireworks.

600 E. Grand Ave.
312-595-7437
www.navypier.org

Play: Centennial Wheel

An iconic and long-standing part of the Chicago skyline, the Centennial Wheel reaches nearly 200 feet high, giving riders panoramic views from the top. Afterward, choose from one of the 36 hand-painted animals and ride the carousel. Thrill seekers will love the Drop Tower, Pepsi Wave Swinger, and Light Tower.

600 E. Grand Ave.
800-595-7437
www.navypier.org

Discover: Chicago Shakespeare Theater

Experience dynamic plays, musicals, family productions, and theatrical presentations at this award-winning, year-round theater, founded in 1986. The Chicago Shakespeare Theater partners with Chicago public schools. Each summer, folks enjoy free Chicago Shakespeare in the parks productions, which happen in neighborhoods across the city.

800 E. Grand Ave.
312-595-5600
www.chicagoshakes.com

Trip Planning:

Streeterville Business Alliance

645 N. Michigan Ave.
312-664-2560
www.streetervillechamber.org

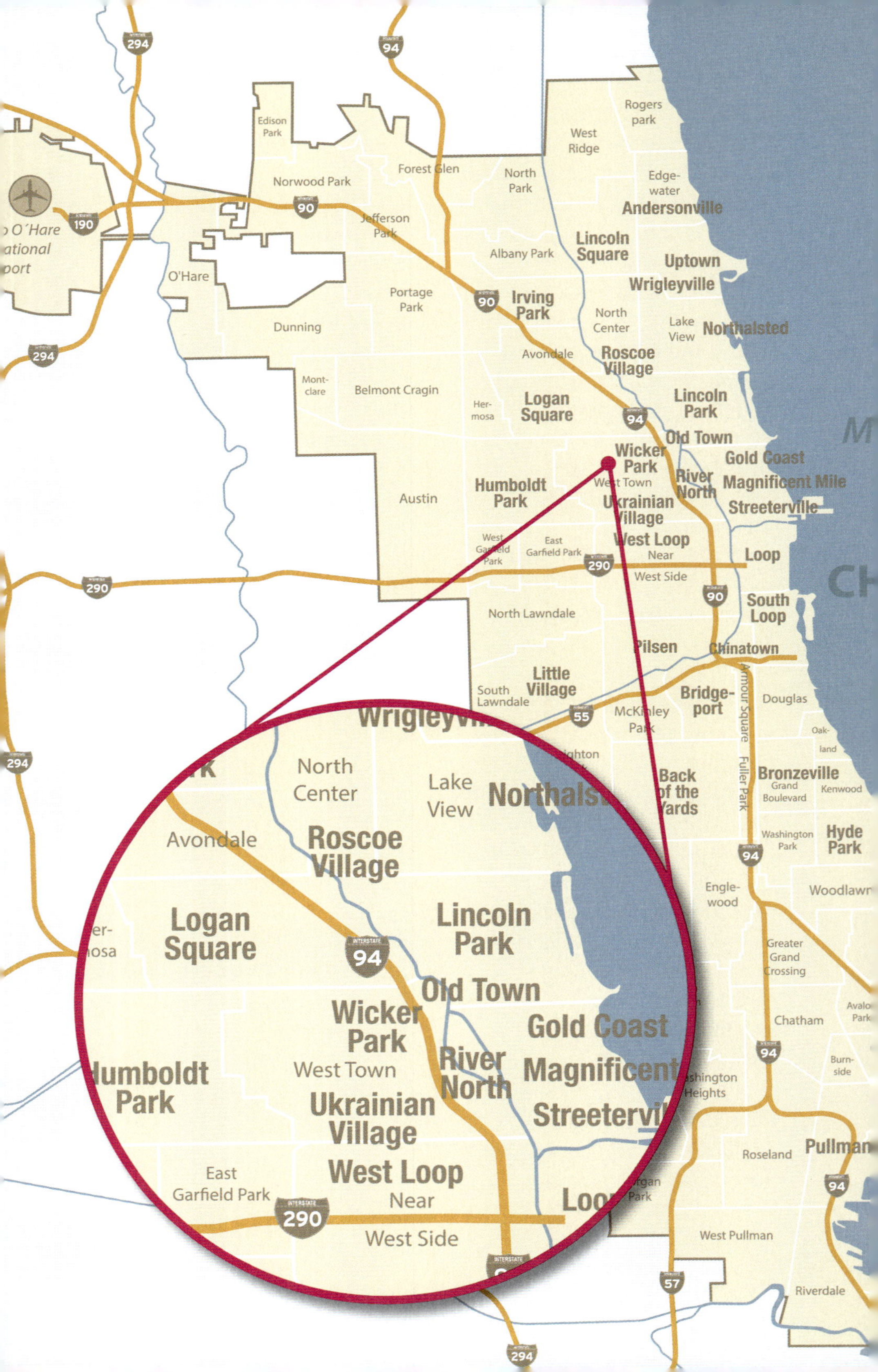

294
94
Edison Park
Rogers park
West Ridge
Edge-water
Andersonville
Forest Glen
North Park
Norwood Park
90
190
Jefferson Park
Albany Park
Lincoln Square
Uptown
Wrigleyville
O'Hare
Portage Park
Irving Park
Dunning
North Center
Lake View
Northalsted
Avondale
Roscoe Village
Mont-clare
Belmont Cragin
Her-mosa
Logan Square
Lincoln Park
Old Town
Wicker Park
West Town
Gold Coast
River North
Magnificent Mile
Austin
Humboldt Park
Ukrainian Village
Streeterville
West Garfield Park
East Garfield Park
West Loop
Near West Side
Loop
290
South Loop
North Lawndale
Pilsen
Chinatown
Little Village
South Lawndale
55
McKinley Park
Bridge-port
Armour Square
Douglas
Oak-land
Back of the Yards
Fuller Park
Bronzeville
Grand Boulevard
Kenwood
Washington Park
Hyde Park
Engle-wood
Woodlawn
Greater Grand Crossing
Chatham
Burn-side
Washington Heights
Roseland
Pullman
Morgan Park
West Pullman
57
Riverdale

WICKER PARK

IRISH, GERMAN, SCANDINAVIAN, Polish, and Jewish immigrants left their marks on Wicker Park, a neighborhood in the West Town community area, and Bucktown, directly north in the Logan Square community area. Begin your day in the famed Six Corners area, known today for being artsy and hipsterish, at the intersections of North, Damen and Milwaukee Avenues. This bustling area is constantly evolving, with plenty of bookstores, coffee shops, ice cream havens, unique eateries, art galleries, and vintage goods.

The Robey, located at Six Corners, offers one of the best views of the city from its 13th-floor lounge, the Up Room. Connecting four Chicago neighborhoods (Wicker Park, Bucktown, Humboldt Park, and Logan Square), the elevated Bloomingdale Trail, home to the 606, is full of art installations and open green space. Its 2.7-mile path is perfect for biking, running, and strolling hand-in-hand. Victorian-style homes, built by wealthy German brewers between 1868 and 1905, can be seen along Hoyne Avenue (once called Beer Baron Row) in the Wicker Park Historic District. It's easy to whittle away the day in this neighborhood.

Margie's Candies

1960 N. Western Ave.
773-348-0400

Part candy store and part ice cream parlor, Margie's Candies, founded in 1921 by a Greek immigrant named Peter George Poulos, is an iconic Chicago staple. Originally named Security Sweet Shop and frequented by the infamous mobster Al Capone, Margie's was run by Poulos' son's wife, Margie, for many decades. In the 1960s, the Beatles ordered "Atomic Sundaes" here, and in the '90s, Liz Phair was photographed here for *Newsweek*.

The real charm of Margie's is not only the history and nostalgia, but also the décor. Not much has changed since the shop first opened. You'll see yellowed newspaper clippings and old black-and-white photographs on the walls, antique Tiffany lamps, a soda fountain, and old-fashioned booths with miniature jukeboxes. Kids who come in with an A on their report card get a free treat. This place, and the ice cream sundaes that come in plastic clamshells, are simply special.

Margie's Candies (Courtesy of Wendy Altschuler)

The Violet Hour (Courtesy of Adam Alexander Photography, Choose Chicago)

The Violet Hour

1520 N. Damen Ave. • 773-252-1500 • www.thevioletthour.com

✔ The James Beard Award–winning artisanal cocktail haven, the Violet Hour, is a must for those interested in a swanky nightlife experience. It's decidedly difficult to spot, with an ever-changing mural on the exterior and an inconspicuous entryway, but once inside, you'll be transported to a different time, where three interior salons and a dramatic white marble bar await. Order pre-Prohibition style libations and small bites. The à la carte menu features classic Violet Hour shaken cocktails like Part & Parcel and the Riviera as well as stirred favorites like Art of Choke and Polka Dot Negroni. If it's nice outside, reserve the Weekend Patio Experience and enjoy sips at the streetside café.

Want more? Join a cocktail class or curated special event. The Old-Fashioned Experience, for example, includes a short cocktail demo, and the Fireside Experience includes an intimate fireside table for an exclusive two-hour tasting of the House Classics, a flight of three hand-selected concoctions.

Piece Pizzeria and Brewery

1927 W. North Ave. • 773-772-4422 • www.piecechicago.com

✓ Piece, founded in 2001 after the transformation of a roofing garage into a pizzeria, is the kind of restaurant where you'll see locals and visitors all gathered to enjoy tasty food and beer. The beer, produced in small batches in their seven-barrel brewhouse, has won Piece 28 medals at the **World Beer Cup** and the **Great American Beer Festival**, including the Champion Small Brewpub. Beyond beer, which Chicagoans love, Piece serves up a variety of pies, including BBQ pizza, Tomato Pie (cheese-free), New Haven-style Pizza (lots of red sauce, extra olive oil, and parmesan—no mozzarella), Hot Doug's Atomic Sausage, and Honey Butter Fried Chicken Pizza. In fact, if you can dream it, they likely have the topping to add to your pie. Do you want mashed potatoes on your pizza? They can do that. Hand-made meatballs? Yep, that too. Sports fans can catch the game while kids can play a round of pinball.

Piece Pizzeria and Brewery
(Courtesy of Wendy Altschuler)

Nearby Alternatives

Discover: Wicker Park Farmers Market

Get a feel for the neighborhood by wandering around the market. Learn how a sense of community is fostered by meeting local vendors. Sample fresh fruit and vegetables, doughnuts, chocolates, baked goods, and cheese. Listen to live music, bring the kids to story time, or check out the yoga and meditation programming.

1425 N. Damen Ave.
773-384-2672
www.wickerparkbucktown.com

Play: Wicker Park

Bring the kids to this sweet little park with a fountain, playground, dog-friendly area, well-tended garden, and field house. You'll see other families and folks hanging around, relaxing in the sunshine and green space.

Pro Tip: Grab takeout noshes from nearby **Antique Taco**, farmers market–style tacos made from scratch, and enjoy a delicious picnic.

1425 N. Damen Ave.
312-742-7553
www.chicagoparkdistrict.com

Discover: Flat Iron Arts Building

Since the 1980s, this triangular-shaped building has served as an outpost, featuring visual artists and musicians of all styles. Visit on the first Friday of every month to meet local artists and see their work—free. Businesses include **Bizarre Bucktown Walking Tour**, **Dorian's Through the Record Shop**, and **Asrai Garden**.

1579 N. Milwaukee Ave.
312-566-9800
www.flatironarts.com

Shop: Bookstore Hop, Start at Myopic Books

Wicker Park and Bucktown have plenty of bookstores, all with their own flair, offering visitors something different and interesting. From Myopic Books to **Quimby's Bookstore** to **Semicolon Bookstore and Gallery** to **Open Books Logan Square**, you can easily spend an afternoon wandering from one to the next.

1564 N. Milwaukee Ave.
773-862-4882
www.myopicbookstore.com

Trip Planning

Wicker Park Bucktown Chamber of Commerce

1414 N. Ashland Ave.
773-384-2672
www.wickerparkbucktown.com

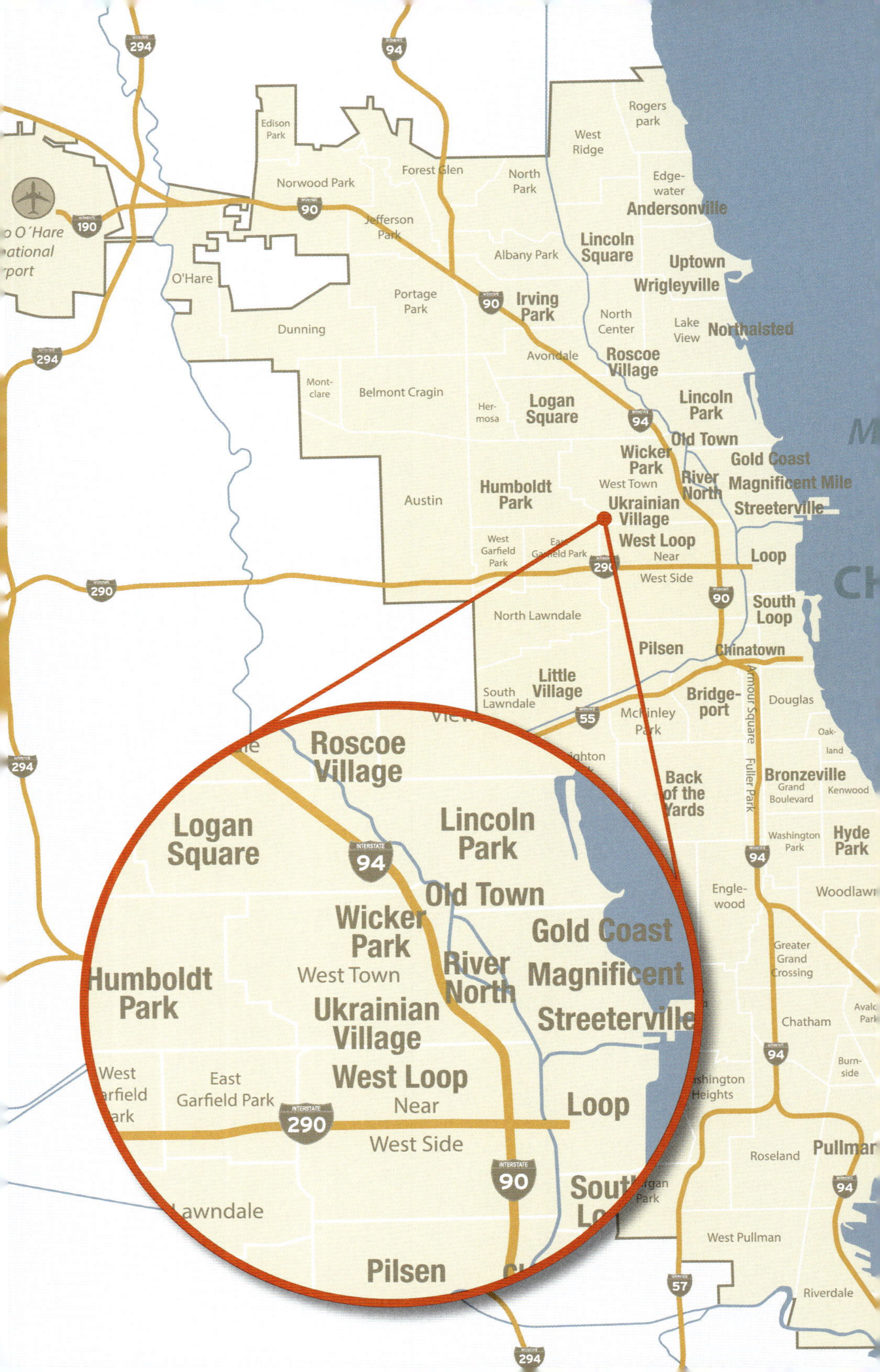

294
94
Rogers park
West Ridge
Edison Park
Forest Glen
North Park
Edge-water
Norwood Park
90
Andersonville
190
Jefferson Park
Lincoln Square
Albany Park
Uptown
O'Hare
Wrigleyville
Portage Park
Irving Park
North Center
Lake View
Northalsted
Dunning
Avondale
Roscoe Village
294
Mont-clare
Belmont Cragin
Her-mosa
Logan Square
Lincoln Park
Old Town
Wicker Park
Gold Coast
West Town
River North
Magnificent Mile
Humboldt Park
Austin
Ukrainian Village
Streeterville
West Garfield Park
West Loop
Loop
Near West Side
290
South Loop
North Lawndale
Pilsen
Chinatown
Little Village
South Lawndale
55
McKinley Park
Bridge-port
Douglas
Armour Square
Oak-land
Back of the Yards
Fuller Park
Bronzeville
Grand Boulevard
Kenwood
Washington Park
Hyde Park
Engle-wood
Woodlawn
Greater Grand Crossing
Chatham
Burn-side
Washington Heights
Roseland
West Pullman
Riverdale
57
Roscoe Village
Logan Square
Lincoln Park
94
Old Town
Wicker Park
Gold Coast
Humboldt Park
West Town
River North
Magnificent
Ukrainian Village
Streeterville
East Garfield Park
West Loop
Near
Loop
290
West Side
90
Lawndale
Pilsen

UKRAINIAN VILLAGE

UKRAINIAN VILLAGE, A vibrant ethnic enclave, is home to one of the largest Ukrainian populations in the country. Situated in the West Town community area, this village, along with neighboring East Village, began as farmland where German Americans once thrived. Since the beginning of the 20th century, Ukrainian cultural identity in Chicago has centered around its churches (St. Nicholas Ukrainian Catholic Cathedral, Sts. Volodymyr and Olha Ukrainian Catholic Parish, and St. Volodymyr Ukrainian Orthodox Cathedral), businesses, schools, and other institutions. However, gentrification of West Town is speedily shifting the demographic. The Ukrainian Village District, which encompasses the oldest part of the neighborhood (1880s), has been designated a Chicago Landmark District.

A visit to this fast-growing locale, full of noteworthy architecture, rewards travelers with the sights, sounds, and tastes of a dynamic culture. From the Ukrainian National Museum to the Ukrainian Cultural Center to the Ukrainian Institute of Modern Art to a plethora of locally owned restaurants, bakeries, and shops, keep reading to discover the top things to experience in this compact community.

Ukrainian National Museum of Chicago

2249 W. Superior St. • 312-421-8020
www.ukrainiannationalmuseum.org

Learn about Ukrainian history and its indelible influence on the city of Chicago at this museum nestled in the heart of the neighborhood. Exhibits include Heritage, Kozak Period, World War I, Chicago's World Fair, Senator Dudycz, Pysanky, Veterans, and Holodomor. The folk-art collection boasts nearly 10,000 items on display. Discover festive, formal, and ritual clothing like the multi-hued patterns of woven and embroidered textiles. A plethora of ceramics, metal, and wooden objects and the large collection of Ukrainian fine art—paintings, drawings, sketches, and sculptures—tell a thought-provoking story. Not to be missed are the Ukrainian Easter eggs, called pysanky, which means "to inscribe." They are covered in traditional folk designs using a wax-resist method. Be sure to visit the gift shop, including the **Children's Corner** and **Children's Books**, to bring home a treasure.

Ukrainian National Museum (Courtesy of Wendy Altschuler)

Black Dog Gelato (Courtesy of Wendy Altschuler)

Black Dog Gelato

859. N. Damen Ave. • 773-235-3116 • www.blackdoggelato.com

✓ After seeing the magnificent cathedrals, sampling noshes from Ukrainian eateries, and visiting folk and fine arts museums, pop into Black Dog Gelato, a light and bright artisanal gelato shop with unconventional flavors like goat cheese cashew caramel, sweet corn, drumstick, and dairy-free Dole whip. Of course, the well-known flavors are also there for the less adventurous. Gelato is churned in the kitchen daily, and once a flavor is gone for the day, it's gone—especially the featured flavors, which rotate monthly.

Jessica Oloroso, a Chicago native and former pastry chef at Stephanie Izard's Scylla, began working on her recipes (she's most proud of her sesame fig chocolate chip recipe) in a shared kitchen in 2007. Black Dog Gelato finally opened its doors in 2010 in Ukrainian Village. It's been featured on Cooking Channel's *Unique Sweets* and FYI Network's *Food Porn*, so it's no surprise that Oloroso's gelato would be regarded as among the best.

Shokolad Pastry & Cafe

2524 W. Chicago Ave. • 773-276-6402 • www.shokoladpastryandcafe.com

✔ If you've never tried Ukrainian dishes before, you're in for a real delight at this well-reviewed European bakery and café that serves up traditional comfort food favorites for breakfast and lunch. Featured on *Check, Please!* and in dozens of local foodie blogs, what started out as a pastry shop has transformed into a vibrant, family-friendly restaurant with beet soup borscht, varenyky, cheese pancakes, pork plov, holubtsi in tomato cream sauce, and hutsulske pechenya on the menu.

Save room for dessert and consider ordering extra sweets to nosh on later. The Napoleon cake goes fast, and for good reason; it's a Shokolad specialty. Other pleasing cake flavors include drunken cherry, honey walnut, ginger lemon, midnight cake, and carrot. And, of course, there are plenty of truffles, cups, parfaits, petit fours, cupcakes, and brownies to choose from. The real treat, however, is the warm welcome you'll receive once you walk through the doors.

Shokolad Pastry & Cafe (Courtesy of Wendy Altschuler)

Nearby Alternatives

Discover: Ukrainian Institute of Modern Art

With education programs and community events that engage audiences through literature, film, music, and art, the Ukrainian Institute of Modern Art is a cornerstone of the community. Part of the **Chicago Cultural Alliance**, this institution promotes and safeguards cultural diversity throughout the Windy City.

2320 W. Chicago Ave.
773-227-5522
www.uima-chicago.org

Discover: Chopin Theater

The award-winning Chopin Theater, initially designed as a nickelodeon, has been serving the community since 1918. Featuring many Eastern and Central European productions as well as performers from all over the globe, Chopin Theater hosts over 500 film, theater, literary, music, and social events annually on its stages and public spaces.

1543 W. Division St.
773-278-1500
www.chopintheater.com

Drink: Dark Matter Coffee Star Lounge

A handful of Dark Matter Coffee shops can be found throughout the city, including two in Ukrainian Village, but the Star Lounge is a standout. Established in 2007, this neighborhood café brings the community together over a well-roasted and brewed cup of java.

2521 W. Chicago Ave.
773-384-7827
www.darkmattercoffee.com

Discover: The Empty Bottle

Musicians like Steven Drozd, drummer of the Flaming Lips, and Tim Nordwind, bassist of OK Go, have frequented the Empty Bottle, a Chicago rock music staple. Owner Bruce Finkelman, co-founder of 16" on Center, describes the Empty Bottle as "a cat-ridden hole-in-the-wall."

1035 N. Western Ave.
773-276-3600
www.emptybottle.com

Trip Planning

Choose Chicago

301 E. Cermak Rd.
312-567-8500
www.choosechicago.com

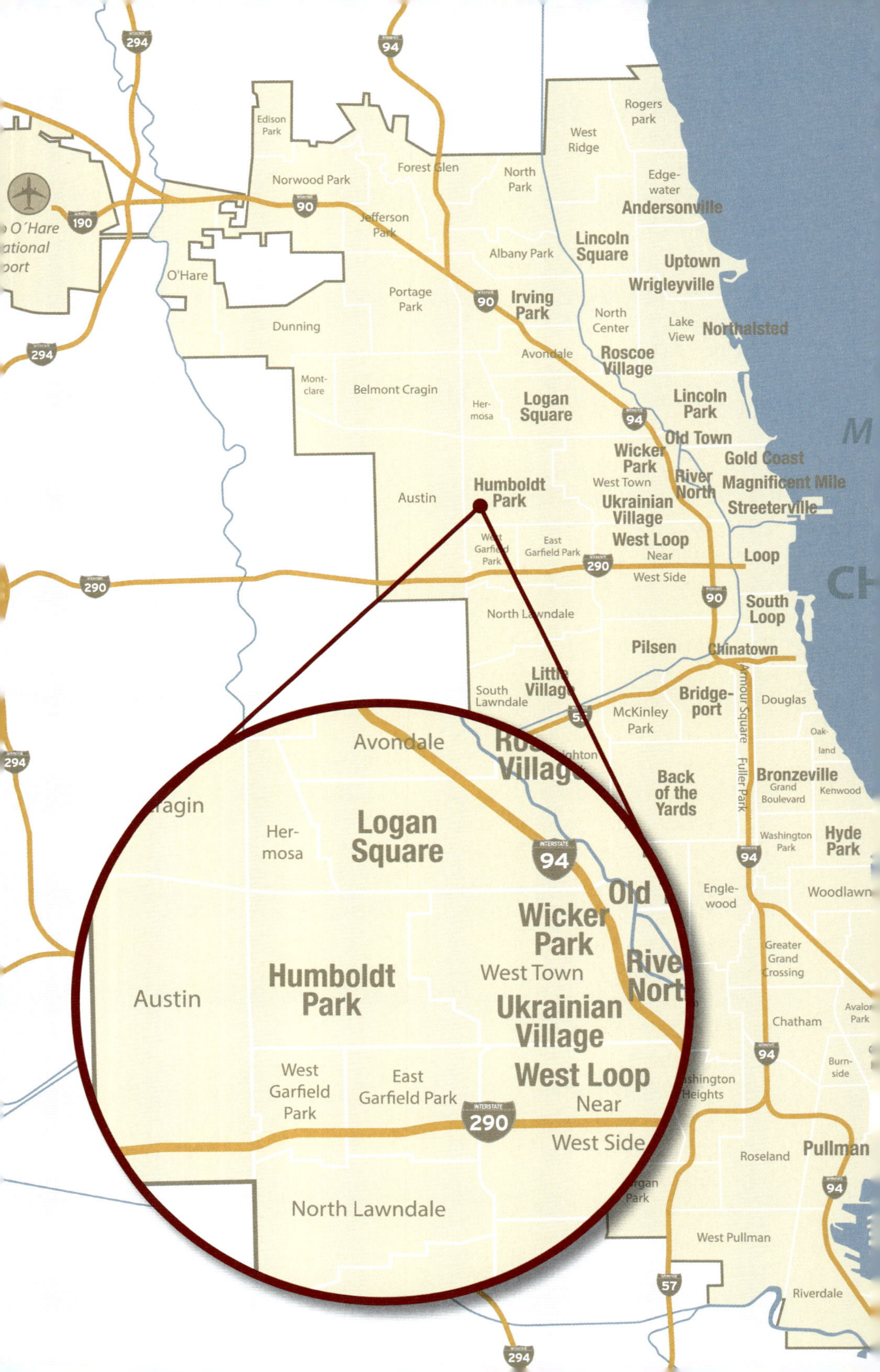

O´Hare International Airport
Edison Park
Norwood Park
Forest Glen
North Park
Rogers park
West Ridge
Edge-water
Andersonville
Jefferson Park
Albany Park
Lincoln Square
Uptown
O'Hare
Portage Park
Irving Park
Wrigleyville
Dunning
North Center
Lake View
Northalsted
Avondale
Roscoe Village
Mont-clare
Belmont Cragin
Her-mosa
Logan Square
Lincoln Park
Old Town
Wicker Park
Gold Coast
River North
Magnificent Mile
West Town
Humboldt Park
Austin
Ukrainian Village
Streeterville
West Garfield Park
East Garfield Park
West Loop
Near West Side
Loop
South Loop
North Lawndale
Pilsen
Chinatown
Little Village
South Lawndale
McKinley Park
Bridge-port
Armour Square
Douglas
Oak-land
Back of the Yards
Fuller Park
Bronzeville
Grand Boulevard
Kenwood
Washington Park
Hyde Park
Engle-wood
Woodlawn
Greater Grand Crossing
Chatham
Avalon Park
Washington Heights
Burn-side
Roseland
Pullman
Morgan Park
West Pullman
Riverdale
294
94
90
190
290
55
57

HUMBOLDT PARK

MASSIVE PUERTO RICAN flags are the gateway to Humboldt Park, one of Chicago's 77 designated community areas. Located on the West Side, Paseo Boricua, a promenade on Division Street, between Western and California Avenues, is where you can see the 59-foot-tall steel flags, a gift from the City of Chicago, flanking each end in this area also known as "Little Puerto Rico." Built in 1995, this public art project—as well as the Puerto Rican Cultural Center and, later, the 606—enlivened the area, engaging locals and visitors with Puerto Rican heritage, and developing Humboldt Park into one of the most exciting Latino neighborhoods in the city.

Along the street, you can discover the walk of fame, with names of prominent Puerto Ricans; businesses named after Puerto Rican towns; and building facades designed after Spanish colonial architecture from old San Juan. Humboldt Park is known for its colorful street art created by local artists; eponymous 200-acre historic park; and several events and festivals, including the multi-day music festival, Riot Fest, so there's oodles to experience here.

Humboldt Park

1440 N. Humboldt Blvd. • 312-742-7549 • www.chicagoparkdistrict.com

Dating back to 1871, Humboldt Park, a substantial green space that features playgrounds, sports courts, nature trails, a lovely lagoon, a meandering river, and the city's only inland beach, is worth a visit. Several events and programs happen here throughout the year, including **Shakespeare in the Park** and **Movies in the Park**. A formal rose garden is protected by two bison statues from the World's Fair, created by the same artist who sculpted the lions in front of the **Art Institute of Chicago**. See the **Alexander Von Humboldt Monument**, which pays tribute to the naturalist and explorer, as well as other outdoor works of art. The historic open-air Prairie-style boat house, built in 1907, has three intricate arches beneath a low-hanging roof—the perfect spot for a family photo. Spend the afternoon grilling and picnicking, wandering the trails, fishing, ordering shaved ice from street vendors, and paddling in the swan-shaped boats.

Humboldt Park (Courtesy of Adam Alexander Photography, Choose Chicago)

National Museum of Puerto Rican Arts and Culture (Courtesy of Abel Arciniega, @tequilagraphics, Choose Chicago)

National Museum of Puerto Rican Arts and Culture

3015 W. Division St. • 773-486-8345 • www.nmprac.org

✔ You might be surprised to learn that the National Museum of Puerto Rican Arts and Culture is the only self-standing national museum in the country focused on Puerto Rican arts and culture. Open year-round, with free parking and admission, the museum provides all residents and sightseers access to its exhibits, so it's easy for families or folks on a budget to visit.

You'll first walk through the historic **Humboldt Park Stables and Receptory Archway**, which will lead you into a brick courtyard with Queen Anne architectural features, fitted with mosaic artwork depicting the island of Puerto Rico. Wander through three different galleries, performance spaces, and arts classrooms, and don't forget to stop in at the unique gift shop. Gain a greater understanding and appreciation of Puerto Rican art and culture through not only the various exhibits, but also the community programming and events, including dynamic arts and crafts festivals, workshops, films, and music.

Kai Zan

2557 W. Chicago Ave. • 773-278-5776
www.eatatkaizan.com

☑ Food from around the globe can be found in Humboldt Park—the options are limitless in this diverse neighborhood. For excellent Japanese-inspired fare, including signature rolls and appetizers, make reservations at Michelin-rated Kai Zan, established in 2012.

Chef and owner siblings Carlo and Melvin Vizconde, known as the sushi twins, are notorious for their Omakase dinner experience. Menu items include char-broil skewers; vegetarian nigiri; oyster shooters; truffle oil-soaked escolar pearls; and pork, beef, or shrimp soba noodles. However, it's best to let the brothers decide what to put on your plate. And, while charming booths are available, you'd be smart to belly right up to the sushi bar so you can see the twins create magic. This unpretentious, compact restaurant, which borders Ukrainian Village, is a true neighborhood gem with plenty of repeat customers.

Oenophiles should wander over to **Rootstock Wine & Beer Bar** afterward to enjoy a praised pour on the patio.

Humboldt Park (Paseo Boricua), nearby, Kai Zan
(Courtesy of Rachel Bires, Choose Chicago)

Nearby Alternatives

Discover: La Casita de Don Pedro

This public art project, created by volunteers, honors the eponymous Puerto Rican nationalist leader. See a replica of a 1940s traditional zinc-roofed rural home, a photo gallery, and a walled garden with a statue of Dr. Pedro Albizu Campos. A small classroom for Plena music performances and workshops is offered to the community.

2625 W. Division St.
773-394-4935
www.paseoboricua.org

Eat: Papa's Cache Sabroso

Family owned and operated, this casual restaurant serves authentic Puerto Rican cuisine like pollo chon, rotisserie chicken with a signature sauce. *Jibaritos*, crispy plantain-based sandwiches (no bread), served with seasoned steak or chicken or made vegetarian, are a Humboldt Park adaptation and fan favorite.

2517 W. Division St.
773-862-8313
www.papascache.com

Discover: Paseo Boricua Tour Company

A great way to learn about Humboldt Park and its history is to take a walking tour with a guide born and raised in the neighborhood. From murals to cultural institutions to eateries, year-round tours will lead you around the six blocks of Division Street (Paseo Boricua) and throughout Humboldt Park.

773-676-5234
www.paseoboricuatours.com

Shop: Humboldt House Co.

Shiny baubles and home goods, vintage finds and art, ceramic treasures and jewelry—find something special, something Chicago-made at this feminist abode of wonder. Need a new planter or set of multi-hued drinkware? They've got it. Candles and sunglasses in every color of the rainbow? Yep, those too.

1045 N. California Ave.
312-785-1442
www.humboldthouseco.com

Trip Planning

Division Street Business Development Association

2459 W. Division St.
773-394-4935
www.paseoboricua.org

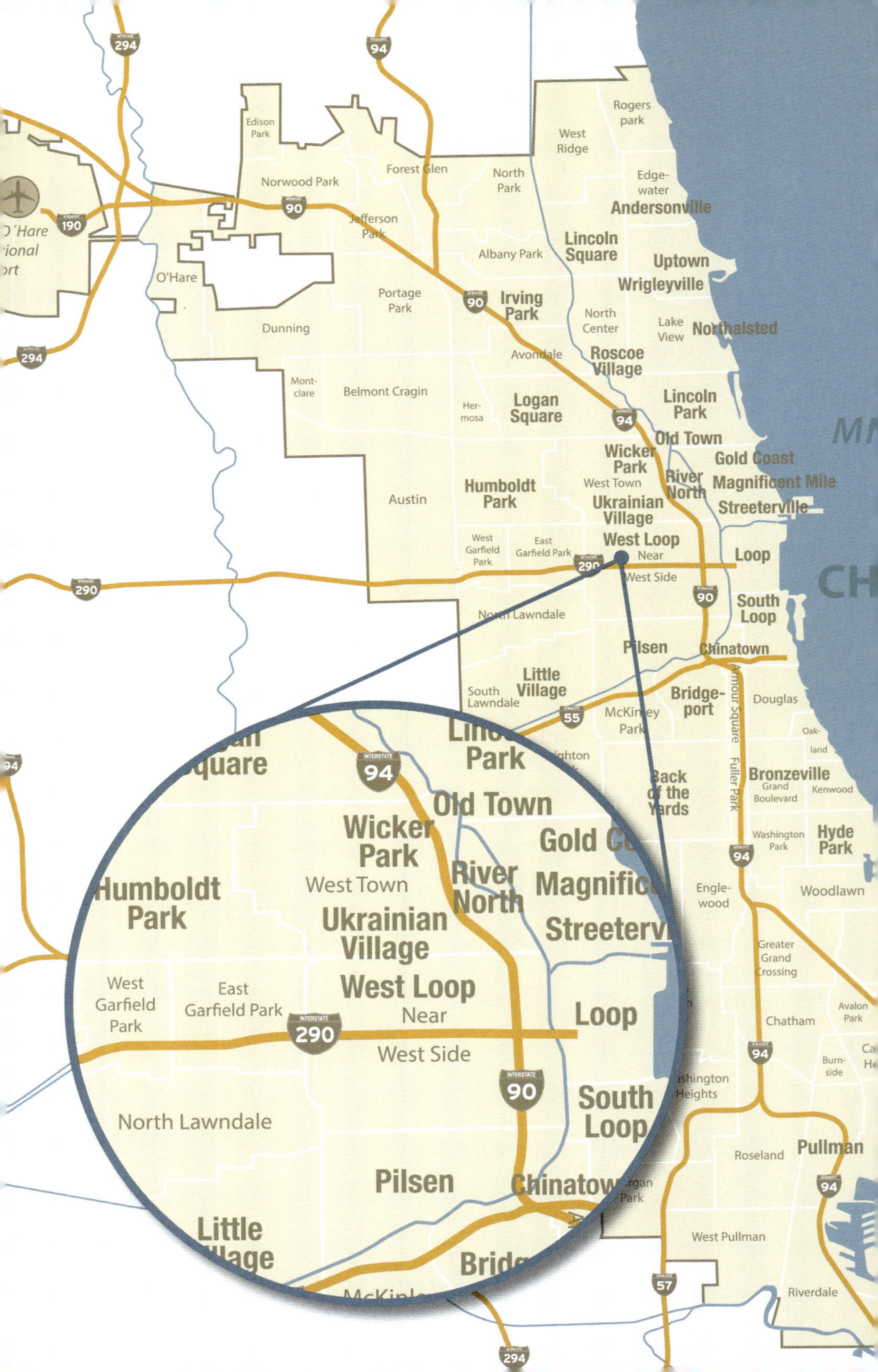

Edison Park
Norwood Park
Forest Glen
North Park
West Ridge
Rogers park
Edgewater
Andersonville
Jefferson Park
O'Hare
Albany Park
Lincoln Square
Uptown
Wrigleyville
Portage Park
Irving Park
North Center
Lake View
Northalsted
Dunning
Avondale
Roscoe Village
Montclare
Belmont Cragin
Hermosa
Logan Square
Lincoln Park
Old Town
Wicker Park
Gold Coast
West Town
River North
Magnificent Mile
Austin
Humboldt Park
Ukrainian Village
Streeterville
West Garfield Park
East Garfield Park
West Loop
Near West Side
Loop
South Loop
North Lawndale
Pilsen
Chinatown
South Lawndale
Little Village
Bridgeport
Armour Square
Douglas
McKinley Park
Back of the Yards
Oakland
Bronzeville
Grand Boulevard
Kenwood
Fuller Park
Washington Park
Hyde Park
Englewood
Woodlawn
Greater Grand Crossing
Avalon Park
Chatham
Burnside
Washington Heights
Roseland
Pullman
Morgan Park
West Pullman
Riverdale
294
94
90
190
290
55
57

WEST LOOP

THE NUCLEUS FOR dining, nightlife, and live music, the West Loop, a former meat-packing district with large industrial warehouses, is where you'll find Michelin-rated eateries along Randolph Street's Restaurant Row, the Chicago French Market, and the historic Union Station, a Beaux-Arts rail hub built in 1925. Hunt for treasures at Randolph Street Market, a European-style flea market. Fulton Market, nearby, is an entertainment district known for global cuisine, coffee shops, breweries, trendy bars, art galleries, and boutique shops that sell indie threads and furnishings. The West Loop is also home to Time Out Market Chicago. Greektown, a vibrant cultural enclave with traditional restaurants, bakeries, delicatessens, and the second-oldest American museum devoted to Greek culture, is nearby. Just west of Skinner and Union parks is the United Center, where the Chicago Bulls and Blackhawks play.

Lovely hotels, most of which have fantastic restaurants, bars, and/or rooftop lounges, include the Hoxton Chicago, Nobu Hotel Chicago, SoHo House Chicago, the Publishing House, and the Emily Hotel.

Chicago French Market

131 N. Clinton St. • 312-575-0306 • www.frenchmarketchicago.com

☑ One level below the **Ogilvie Transportation Center**, Chicago's hub for Metra train lines, sits the year-round indoor **Chicago French Market**, a European-style global marketplace and food hall. An urban gem since 2009, it offers over 30 unique purveyors, including **A Taste of the Philippines**, **Cubano Bros**, **Blue Spot Sushi**, **Kathryn's Soul**, **Olive Mediterranean Grill**, **Saigon Sisters**, **Lito's Empanadas**, **Bangaroos Aussie Pies**, and **Aloha Poke**. At the concourse entrance, you can find the **City Fresh Market** grocery store and **Vanille Patisserie**, home of the city's top French macarons, mousse cakes, tarts, and handmade chocolates and candies. Dog treats and chews can be found at **Barking Spot Bakery and Boutique**. Choose your grab-and-go goods and then sit in the Parisian-style café, with a mural of Paris, or venture outside and snag a patio table. With so many independent selections, everyone in your crew is certain to find something to enjoy.

Chicago French Market (Courtesy of Wendy Altschuler)

Randolph Street Market (Courtesy of Tina Malek)

Randolph Street Market

1341 W. Randolph St. • 312-666-1199 • www.randolphstreetmarket.com

A great way to not only rub elbows with Chicagoans but also find unique treasures is to visit the Randolph Street Market, one of the most popular bazaars in the country. Housed at **Chicago's Plumbers Hall**, it's a great place to wander from booth to booth and marvel at all the vintage, modern, and designer goods. At America's biggest and boldest urban antique market, you can shop while meeting artists and vendors from around the country. Unique gems include vintage quilts; pottery; steampunk lighting; vinyl; handmade shoes, clothing, and jewelry; vintage cowboy hats and boots; rare novels and magazines; African art, artifacts, and textiles; home décor; and bespoke poetry. A roster of live music will keep you entertained as you shop during the outdoor **Randolph Street Market Festival**. The festival is home to the **Chicago Antique Market**, a monthly indoor/outdoor flea market; **Indie Designer Market**, for emerging fashion talent; and the annual **Holiday Market**.

Girl & the Goat

809 W. Randolph St. • 312-492-6262 • www.girlandthegoat.com

☑ Chicagoans rave about Girl & the Goat, Executive Chef Stephanie Izard's original restaurant with Boka Restaurant Group and one of the first to open on Restaurant Row. Izard, a *Top Chef* Season Four winner, opened the award-winning 122-seat perennial hot spot in 2010 and has been serving family-style favorites—meat, fish, and vegetables—ever since. The ambience is warm and inviting, with wooden furniture and bold art. Izard is a partner at three other Chicago restaurants—**Little Goat**, **Duck Duck Goat**, and **Cabra Cevicheria**, and has been awarded multiple "Best Chef" titles.

Bring the experience home with cooking sauces and spices from Izard's product line, "This Little Goat," and pick up copies of her books *Girl in the Kitchen* and *Gather & Graze* to recreate recipes at your leisure.

Girl & The Goat (Courtesy of Wendy Altschuler)

Nearby Alternatives

Play: Brooklyn Boulders

Burn off some energy—especially since you've been eating your way around the West Loop—and romp around at Brooklyn Boulders, an indoor climbing gym. Climbing classes for beginners through advanced levels are available. Traveling with little ones in tow? Youth programming is offered for ages five and up.

100 S. Morgan St.
312-268-0002
www.brooklynboulders.com

Discover: National Hellenic Museum

Founded in the early '80s, this four-story museum preserves Greek culture, history, and heritage through community events and programs, artifacts that span thousands of years, and hundreds of oral history interviews. The exhibit "Reaching for the American Dream: The Greek Story in America" features photos, stories, and objects that convey the Greek American experience.

333 S. Halsted St.
312-655-1234
www.nationalhellenicmuseum.org

Play: Union Park

This city park, created in 1853 and covering nearly 14 acres, hosts special events throughout the year like Night Out in the Parks concerts, outdoor movie screenings, and the Pitchfork Music Festival. A field house, plenty of sports courts, a playground, and a swimming pool keep folks busy, especially during the summer months.

1501 W. Randolph St.
312-746-5494
www.chicagoparkdistrict.com

Play: WNDR Museum

Art reigns supreme at WNDR Museum, an immersive experience with a variety of interesting exhibits including the Yayoi Kusama Infinity Room, WNDR Light Floor, and Ames (an optical illusion). Move from one room to another through interesting works created by provocative artists, and challenge yourself to think more deeply about the themes explored in the exhibits.

1130 W. Monroe St.
www.wndrmuseum.com

Trip Planning

Choose Chicago

72 E. Randolph St.
312-567-8500
www.choosechicago.com

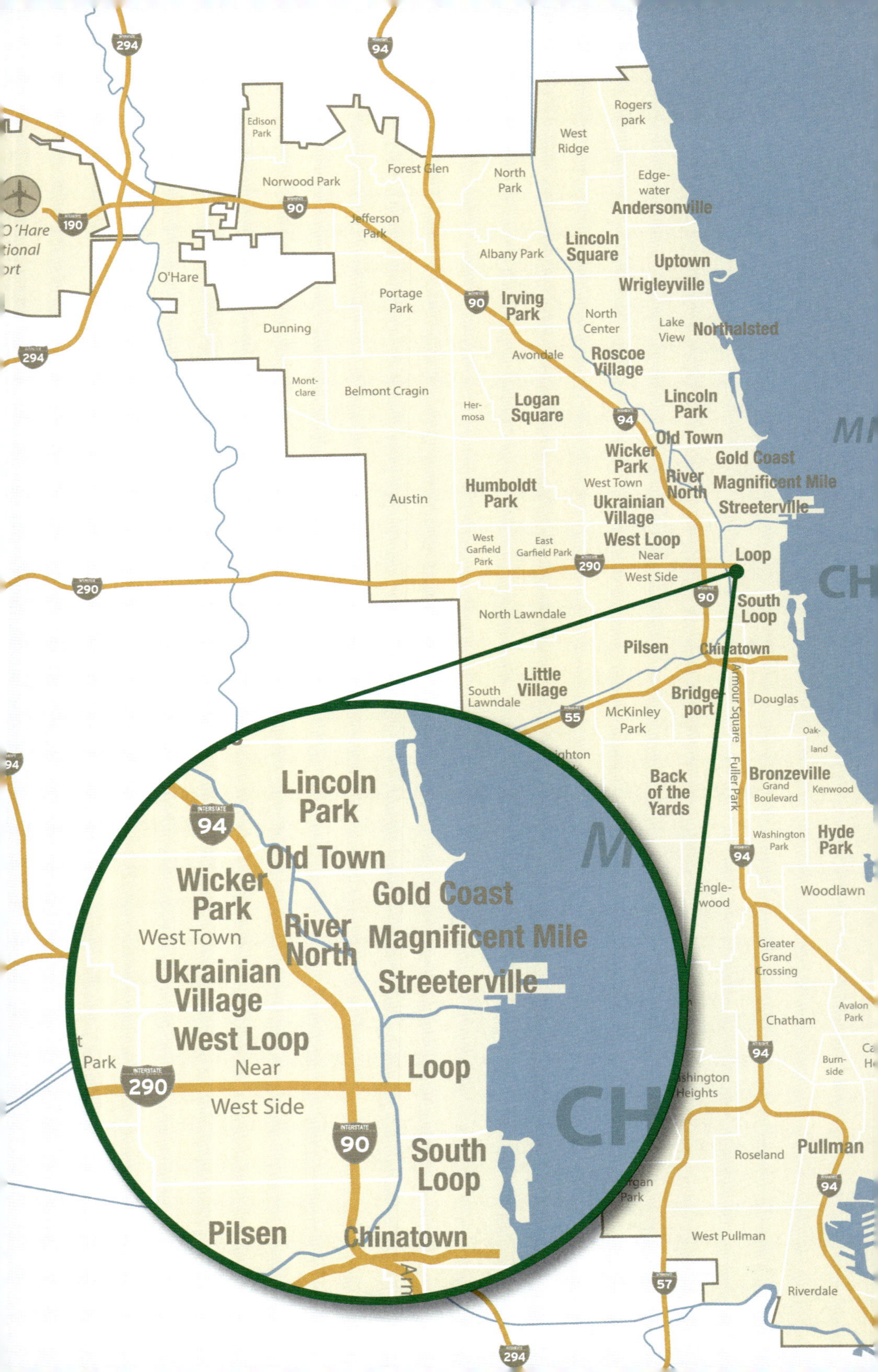

294
94
Edison Park
Rogers park
West Ridge
Edge-water
Andersonville
Norwood Park
Forest Glen
North Park
190
90
Jefferson Park
Albany Park
Lincoln Square
Uptown
Wrigleyville
O'Hare
Portage Park
Irving Park
North Center
Lake View
Northalsted
Dunning
Avondale
Roscoe Village
Mont-clare
Belmont Cragin
Her-mosa
Logan Square
Lincoln Park
Old Town
Wicker Park
West Town
River North
Gold Coast
Magnificent Mile
Streeterville
Austin
Humboldt Park
Ukrainian Village
West Loop
West Garfield Park
East Garfield Park
290
Near West Side
Loop
South Loop
North Lawndale
Pilsen
Chinatown
Little Village
South Lawndale
55
McKinley Park
Bridge-port
Armour Square
Douglas
Oak-land
Back of the Yards
Fuller Park
Bronzeville
Grand Boulevard
Kenwood
Washington Park
Hyde Park
Engle-wood
Woodlawn
Greater Grand Crossing
Chatham
Avalon Park
Burn-side
Roseland
Pullman
West Pullman
57
Riverdale

LOOP

THE LOOP, CHICAGO'S official downtown, is chock-full of things to explore, from galleries and museums to pop-up attractions, gardens and parks, music and theater, landmarks, and public art. Hop aboard Chicago's First Lady, with the Chicago Architecture Center, and learn about some of the city's most important buildings along the Chicago River and Chicago Riverwalk. Visit Millennium Park and see Cloud Gate, also known as "the Bean"; Crown Fountain; Lurie Garden; and the Jay Pritzker Pavilion, where the Chicago Jazz Festival, Chicago Blues Festival, and a free summer music and film series are held annually. Maggie Daley Park has a climbing wall, skating ribbon, mini golf, and imaginative play garden. The Chicago Cultural Center is not only a beautiful landmark building, with the world's largest Tiffany-stained glass dome, but also the site of free exhibits, concerts, and performances. Skydeck in Willis Tower is a top attraction for both the panoramic skyline views and also the Ledge, a glass box you can stand in that extends outside the building.

Self-led Architecture Tour, Begin at St. Regis Chicago (Vista Tower)

363 E. Wacker Dr. • 203-980-9688
www.studiogang.com/project/vista-tower

✔ The world's first skyscraper was erected in Chicago in 1885. Groundbreaking architects Ludwig Mies van der Rohe, Louis Sullivan, Daniel Burnham, and Frank Lloyd Wright painted the skyline with structural masterpieces.

Innovation continues today with **Aqua Tower** and St. Regis Chicago (the city's third-tallest building). Both are located in the city's newest neighborhood, **New Eastside**, and they are the two tallest structures in the world designed by a lead female architect, Jeanne Gang.

Next, travel to **Chicago City Hall**, where a green roof has been planted. See the Art Deco and Art Nouveau **Civic Opera House**; **Willis Tower**, known locally as **Sears Tower**; the **Rookery Building**, the oldest standing high-rise in Chicago; **Marquette Building**, a Chicago landmark, decorated with a mosaic frieze in the atrium; the **Fisher Building**, a neo-Gothic landmark with carvings of aquatic creatures on its facade; **Harold Washington Library**, with the Winter Garden's glass ceiling; and the **Fine Arts Building**, designed for working artists.

Architecture Tour (Courtesy of Wendy Altschuler)

Downtown Theater District (Courtesy of Choose Chicago)

Downtown Theater District/League of Chicago Theaters

17 N. Wabash St. • 312-554-9800
www.chicagoplays.com

☑ Visit the Chicago Theater District and see a performance at the **Auditorium Theatre**, the **Chicago Symphony Orchestra**, the **Chicago Theatre**, the **Gene Siskel Film Center**, the Tony Award-winning **Goodman Theatre** (Chicago's oldest and largest not-for-profit theater), the **Joffrey Ballet**, **Lyric Opera of Chicago**, or **Silk Road Rising**. **Broadway in Chicago** showcases pre-Broadway productions, entertaining 1.7 million guests each year in its five theaters: **Cadillac Palace Theatre**, an ornate venue inspired by the **Palace of Versailles**; **CIBC Theatre**, which first opened as a vaudeville theater in 1906; **James M. Nederlander Theatre**, a lavish movie palace from the early 1900s; **Auditorium Theatre**, a National Historic Landmark; and **Broadway Playhouse** at Water Tower Place. Broadway in Chicago also offers history tours at select theaters. The League of Chicago Theatres, founded in 1979, serves more than 200 playhouses. Explore show listings, learn about the different theaters, and purchase discounted tickets through the website's Hot Tix.

Cindy's Rooftop Restaurant

12 S. Michigan Ave. • 312-792-3502 • www.cindysrooftop.com

✓ Don't even think about trying to get a table at Cindy's Rooftop Restaurant without a reservation, no matter what season. It's located above Michigan Avenue, on top of the **Chicago Athletic Association**, which is also worth a visit for its Venetian Gothic architecture (1893), dark and cozy drawing room, lively game room, and events at **Stagg Court**. Cindy's has some of the best views of **Millennium Park**, **Lake Michigan**, and the **Art Institute of Chicago** from its terrace.

The family-style New American comfort fare is delectable, beginning with chia bowls, house salads, and sandwiches for brunch and finishing with burrata, whole grilled fish, and a grasshopper ice cream sandwich for dinner. With a glass and steel vaulted rooftop and a casual-yet-luxe beach-house vibe, this is the spot to enjoy an expertly crafted cocktail or mocktail or a glass of biodynamic wine. (**Acanto**, the **Gage**, and **Hot Woks Cool Sushi** are fantastic choices nearby.)

Cindy's Rooftop Restaurant
(Courtesy of Nick Gerber)

Nearby Alternatives

Discover: Art Institute of Chicago

The Art Institute is one of the world's top museums, with works from around the globe, including the largest collection of Impressionist paintings outside of Paris. See works by Seurat, Monet, Picasso, Van Gogh, O'Keeffe, and Matisse. Visit the **Thorne Miniature Rooms**, the medieval arms and armor collection, and the light-filled modern wing.

111 S. Michigan Ave.
312-443-3600
www.artic.edu

Discover: Clarence Buckingham Memorial Fountain

In the heart of **Grant Park** sits the Beaux Arts Buckingham Fountain, representing Lake Michigan with four sets of seahorses that symbolize the bordering states—Illinois, Wisconsin, Michigan, and Indiana. For 20 minutes each hour, a jet shoots water 150 feet into the air; at dusk, lights accompany the display.

301 S. Columbus Dr.
312-742-3918
www.chicagoparkdistrict.com

Discover: Daley Plaza

The granite civic plaza, used for festivals and cultural events, is where you'll find the colossal Chicago Picasso. A gift from the artist, the sculpture appears in several major movies including *The Blues Brothers*, *The Fugitive*, *Ferris Bueller's Day Off*, and *The Dark Knight*. Visit farmers markets, food trucks, and the German-inspired **Christkindlmarket**.

50 W. Washington St.
312-603-5030
www.thedaleycenter.com

Discover: Museum of Contemporary Photography

Founded by Columbia College Chicago in 1976, and accredited by the American Alliance of Museums, MoCP is an inspiring free museum devoted to photography. Exhibitions demonstrate how photos can shape cultural and political perspectives. Afterward, visit the lovely **Spirit of Music Gardens** nearby in **Grant Park**.

600 S. Michigan Ave.
312-663-5554
www.mocp.org

Trip Planning

Chicago Loop Alliance

55 W. Monroe St.
312-782-9160
www.loopchicago.com

294
94
Edison Park
Rogers park
West Ridge
Forest Glen
North Park
Edge-water
Norwood Park
Andersonville
90
Jefferson Park
O´Hare
190
Lincoln Square
Albany Park
Uptown
O'Hare
Wrigleyville
Portage Park
Irving Park
North Center
Lake View
Northalsted
Dunning
Avondale
Roscoe Village
294
Mont-clare
Belmont Cragin
Lincoln Park
Her-mosa
Logan Square
Old Town
Wicker Park
Gold Coast
Humboldt Park
West Town
River North
Magnificent Mile
Austin
Ukrainian Village
Streeterville
West Garfield Park
East Garfield Park
West Loop
Near
Loop
290
West Side
South Loop
North Lawndale
Pilsen
Chinatown
Little Village
South Lawndale
55
McKinley Park
Bridge-port
Douglas
Armour Square
Fuller Park
Oak-land
Back of the Yards
Bronzeville
Grand Boulevard
Kenwood
Washington Park
Hyde Park
Engle-wood
Woodlawn
Greater Grand Crossing
Avalon Park
Chatham
Burn-side
Washington Heights
Roseland
Pullman
Morgan Park
West Pullman
57
Riverdale
294

SOUTH LOOP

THE SOUTH LOOP is located (sorry to ruin the surprise) south of the Loop. Here, nestled along the waterfront and adjacent to Northerly Island, you'll find Museum Campus, which includes five of the city's most prominent attractions: Adler Planetarium, Shedd Aquarium, the Field Museum, Soldier Field, and McCormick Place.

It's not all museums, however. Many folks have heard of Chicago's Gold Coast, but what about the Prairie Avenue Historic District, home of the Glessner House? It's a National Historic Landmark where horseback riders and carriages once made their way past a dense cluster of "Millionaire Row" mansions belonging to the city's well-heeled, including George Pullman and Marshall Field.

Today, only a handful of original mansions stand, but you can see the Clark House, Chicago's oldest house (built in 1836), now located in the district's Chicago Women's Park and Garden. Hugging the lakefront, Grant Park, known as Chicago's front yard, is home to public art, the Lakefront Trail, and the city's biggest events and festivals, like Taste of Chicago, the Grant Park Music Festival, the Chicago Marathon, and Lollapalooza.

Adler Planetarium

1300 S. DuSable Lake Shore Dr. • 312-922-7827 • www.adlerplanetarium.org

✓ America's first planetarium, Adler Planetarium was popular during the 1933–34 World's Fair. Walk through the entrance, Rainbow Lobby, and see multi-hued sweeps of color created through glass prisms. Sit inside the **Atwood Sphere** during a live guided tour and learn about the stars that form popular constellations. Kids love the **Clark Family Welcome Gallery**, home to pop-up exhibits and always-changing scenery. Test your ideas, create, and learn through hands-on science and art at the **Community Design Labs**. Wander through Our Solar System and see colossal models of Saturn, Jupiter, Neptune, and Uranus as well as a real meteorite.

Beyond exhibits, you can delight in award-winning sky shows in the dome theater and special events like Adler at Night. Don't skip the outdoor terrace, complete with a 13-foot working sundial; **Doane Observatory**, Chicago's largest public telescope, where you can see celestial objects trillions of miles away; and arguably the best views of the Chicago skyline.

Adler Planetarium (Courtesy of Wendy Altschuler)

Field Museum
(Courtesy of Field Museum, Lucy Hewett)

Field Museum

1400 S. DuSable Lake Shore Dr.
312-922-9410 • www.fieldmuseum.org

The Field Museum has 40 million artifacts and specimens in its collection. Learn about cultures from around the globe as well as the latest scientific discoveries through the diverse exhibits, movies, and labs.

Experience Native American life in the **Pawnee Earth Lodge**; see Sue the T-Rex at **Griffin Halls of Evolving Planet**; marvel at precious stones at **Granger Hall of Gems**; examine soil and science 1/100th of your size at **Underground Adventure**; descend into a tomb and peek at human and animal mummies and hieroglyphs at **Inside Ancient Egypt**; and see Maximo the Titanosaur, the largest dinosaur ever to walk the earth, at **Stanley Field Hall**. Watch real scientists at work in the **DNA Discovery Center** and be sure to take part in one of the many special events like lectures, poetry pop-ups, and scientist talks. Don't skip the outdoors—the **Rice Native Gardens** has over 100 native plants, grasses, and flowers.

Fatpour Tap Works

2206 S. Indiana Ave. • 312-878-9292 • www.fatpourmccormick.com

✓ **Motor Row** is one of the city's newest fun havens. Once lined with historic buildings built between 1905 and 1936 on Michigan Avenue, where a variety of automobiles were sold and repaired, the strip has now been designated as an entertainment and dining district in the **McCormick Place** area. Instead of car showrooms, visitors can experience theater, restaurant, bar, hotel, and retail magic. Eatery options include **Lips**, for dinner and a drag show; **Il Culacinno**, for Italian favorites; **VU**, a trendy rooftop bar with stellar views; **14 Parish**, for Caribbean fusion fare; and Fatpour, a sport's bar and restaurant.

The largest beer venue in the South Loop, Fatpour has a little bit of everything on its menu, making it ideal for families and groups. Try anything from pasta to chicken 'n waffles, salads, pizzas, burgers, and shareable "fat plates," and enjoy the patio—or, if the weather is iffy, grab a table by the keg wall.

Fatpour (Courtesy of Fatpour McCormick)

Nearby Alternatives

Discover: Shedd Aquarium

The Water Taxi can drop you at Shedd Aquarium, home to Abbott Oceanarium, Amazon Rising, Caribbean Reef, Wild Reef, Polar Play Zone, and Island and Lakes exhibits as well as animal encounters and 4-D shows. See sharks, otters, jellyfish, fresh and saltwater fish, penguins, sea horses, stingrays, beluga whales, and dolphins.

1200 S. DuSable Lake Shore Dr.
312-939-2438
www.sheddaquarium.org

Discover: Dearborn Station and Printers Row

Once a printing hub circa 1880, Printers Row is now a neighborhood home to **Sandmeyer's Bookstore**, a farmers market at **Printers Row Park**, **Printers Row Wine Bar and Shop**, **Roots Handmade Pizza**, the **Printers Row Lit Fest**, and Dearborn Station, the city's oldest railroad station, which is now a marketplace near **Dearborn Park**.

47 W. Polk St.
312-554-8100
www.dearbornstation.com

Discover: Buddy Guy's Legends

Sandwiched between **Grant Park** and **Printers Row**, Buddy Guy's Legends is a Chicago staple for year-round blues music. Rock and Roll Hall of Famer Buddy Guy performs in January. Cajun and soul food favorites include gumbo, po' boys, fried chicken with Buffalo sauce, cornbread, and key lime pie.

700 S. Wabash Ave.
312-427-1190
www.buddyguy.com

Discover: Wabash Arts Corridor

One of the largest community-driven public art collectives in the country, Wabash Arts Corridor was founded in 2013 by **Columbia College** Chicago. It has transformed urban spaces along Wabash Avenue into a vibrant outdoor art museum, with dozens of murals in alleys and parking lots and on building facades.

635 S. Wabash Ave.
www.wabashartscorridor.org

Trip Planning

Chicago Loop Alliance

55. W. Monroe St.
312-782-9160
www.loopchicago.com

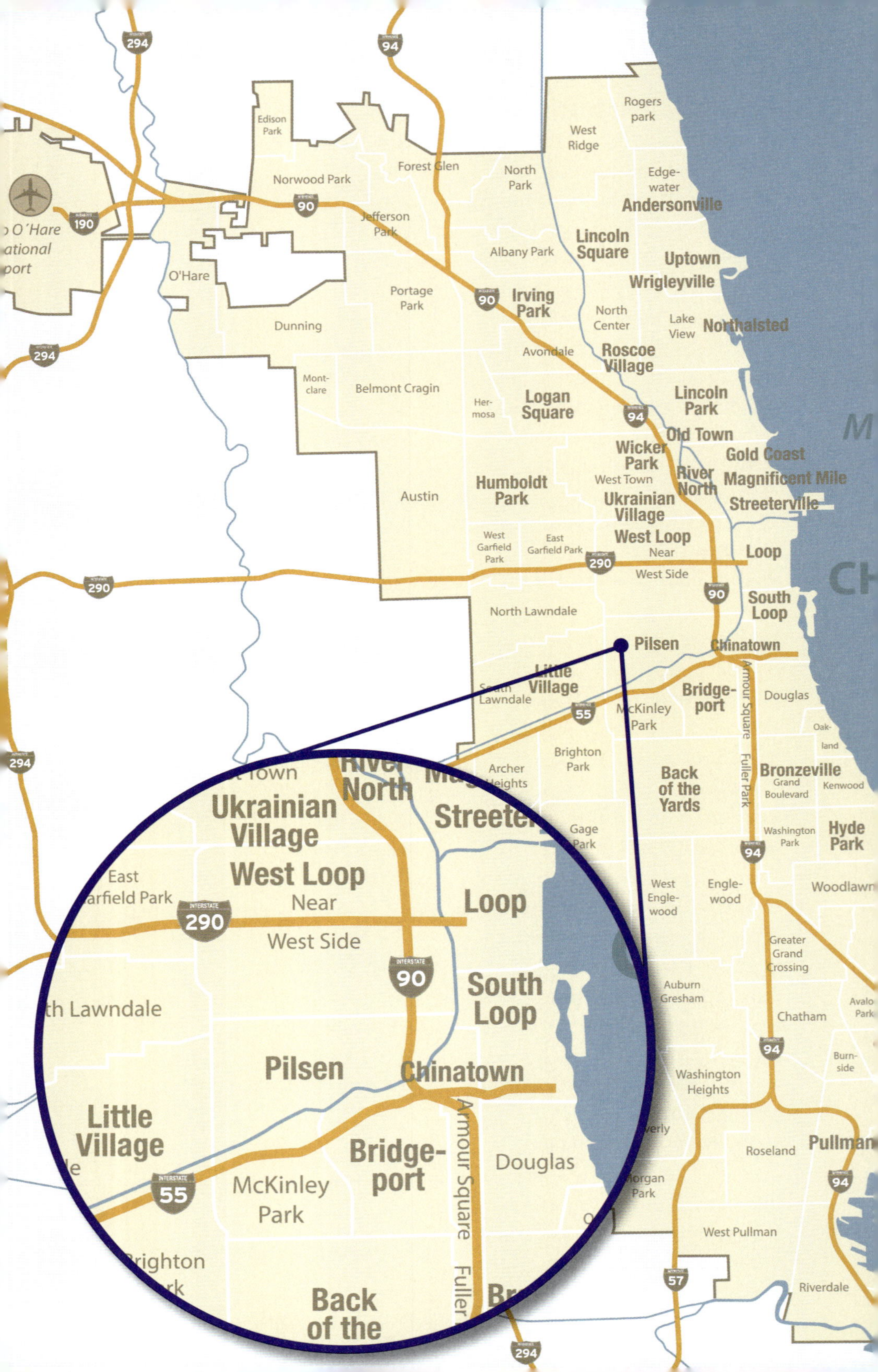

O'Hare International Airport
Edison Park
Norwood Park
Forest Glen
North Park
West Ridge
Rogers park
Edge-water
Andersonville
Jefferson Park
Albany Park
Lincoln Square
Uptown
Wrigleyville
O'Hare
Portage Park
Irving Park
North Center
Lake View
Northalsted
Dunning
Avondale
Roscoe Village
Mont-clare
Belmont Cragin
Her-mosa
Logan Square
Lincoln Park
Old Town
Wicker Park
Gold Coast
West Town
River North
Magnificent Mile
Austin
Humboldt Park
Ukrainian Village
Streeterville
West Garfield Park
East Garfield Park
West Loop
Near West Side
Loop
South Loop
North Lawndale
Pilsen
Chinatown
Little Village
South Lawndale
Bridge-port
Armour Square
Douglas
McKinley Park
Oak-land
Archer Heights
Brighton Park
Back of the Yards
Fuller Park
Bronzeville
Grand Boulevard
Kenwood
Gage Park
Washington Park
Hyde Park
West Engle-wood
Engle-wood
Woodlawn
Greater Grand Crossing
Auburn Gresham
Chatham
Avalon Park
Burn-side
Washington Heights
Beverly
Pullman
Roseland
Morgan Park
West Pullman
Riverdale

PILSEN

THOUGH PILSEN, LOCATED on the Lower West Side, was founded by Irish and German immigrants, Czechs settled in the area after the Great Chicago Fire, establishing landmarks like the St. Procopius Church and Thalia Hall. Mexican families made homes in this pride-filled neighborhood in the mid-1900s, and even though new businesses and residents from diverse cultures are currently moving in, Hispanic cuisine, music, art, and shops still brighten the community.

You'll notice the multicolored street art right away—on buildings, in alleyways, wrapped around train platforms and railway overpasses, and even on houses. The 16th Street Murals, unfolding on an old railroad embankment from Halsted Street to Western Avenue, features art from renowned artists like JC Rivera, Sam Kirk, Chris Silva, Amuse, Roa, and Hebru Brantley. Women Made Gallery is a space for women and nonbinary artists to showcase their work. The Pilsen Arts and Community House functions as a nonprofit art gallery and community center. Mana Contemporary Chicago is home to artist studios, a library, and exhibition spaces. Here, art is king.

National Museum of Mexican Art

1852 W. 19th St. • 312-738-1503
www.nationalmuseumofmexicanart.org

✓ Founded in 1982, the free-to-all National Museum of Mexican Art represents the Mexican community through its permanent art collection, performing arts and cultural programs, community education, and special events. Formerly the Mexican Fine Arts Center Museum, the institution and audience have expanded, calling for a larger facility nestled in Harrison Park, in the heart of Pilsen. Home to America's largest Mexican art collection, this is the first Latino Museum accredited by **American Alliance of Museums**.

From pop art to textiles, paintings, sculptures, and photography, there's much to see here. Experience live dance and theater, hear music, and take part in children's and family programming. Don't skip the gift shop, **Tienda Tzintzuntzan**, or "place of the hummingbird," for art, textiles, jewelry, toys, and books—it's one of the best in the city. While food and drinks aren't available, nearby gems worth a visit include **5 Rabanitos**, **Las Carnitas Urupan**, and **La Mejikana**.

National Museum of Mexican Art (Courtesy of Graham Chapman, Choose Chicago)

Thalia Hall (Courtesy of Powell Photography, Choose Chicago)

Thalia Hall

1807 S. Allport St. • 312-526-3851
www.thaliahallchicago.com

Modeled after the Prague opera house, Thalia Hall, a gorgeous historic landmark building in the heart of Pilsen, was founded by John Dusek in 1892. It operated as a community public hall with storefronts, housing, and an opulent theater. In 2013, owners Bruce Finkelman and Craig Golden created five imaginative spaces with nods to the building's history and the neighborhood's roots: Thalia Hall, a haven for live performers and artists; **Dusek's Tavern**, presenting delectable menu items and drinks; **Tack Room**, a charming cocktail bar that once housed Dusek's horses; **Punch House**, set in the basement and offering modern shareable punches and late-night fun; and the **Beer Cellar**, a private dining space sited under Dusek's Tavern behind a revolving bookcase. Unless noted, all shows at the Thalia Hall complex are appropriate for all ages. Nearby, **La Michoacana Premium** is the "it" place to go for iced sweet treats.

Pilsen Yards

1163 W. 18th St. • 312-243-2410 • www.pilsenyards.com

☑ Tasty Latin street food like handmade tacos, sweet corn tamales, and piña colada ceviche are on the menu at this music-driven hidey-hole. Open for brunch and dinner, Pilsen Yards, with its affordable fare and alfresco vibe, is a neighborhood win. Rebranded from the former Monnie Burke's, the indoor/outdoor speakeasy-inspired patio is a jovial place to see dynamic art shows, listen to live music on Thursday nights, or hear vinyl DJ sets on the weekends.

The well-warmed patio space, with a poured-cement heated floor, see-through roof, ambient lighting, and exposed brick and wooden beams, is open year-round. Not to be overlooked, the **Alderman**, an award-winning, upscale, 16-seat bar located at the back of the restaurant, is intimate and ideal for a nightcap. Good food, good drinks, and an even better unpretentious community vibe is what it's all about at Pilsen Yards.

Pilsen Yards (Courtesy of Sammy Faze Photography)

Nearby Alternatives

Shop: Pilsen Community Books

Founded in 2016, this employee-owned and operated independent bookstore offers a monthly book subscription program, community events, and a plethora of staff recommendations. The long-standing literacy program, Pilsen Reads, cultivates the love of books in neighborhood youth. Pop in, pick up a hardcover, tote, and t-shirt, and enjoy this light-filled space.

1102 W. 18th St.
312-478-9434
www.pilsencommunitybooks.com

Drink: Café Jumping Bean

This community-driven coffee house and gallery has been a neighborhood staple since 1994. Whether you're staying for casual noshes; quickly grabbing an iced coffee on the way to nearby vintage shops like **Pilsen Vintage**, **Very Best Vintage**, or **Knee Deep Vintage**; or en route to **Semillas Plant Studio**, you'll love a sojourn here.

1439 W. 18th St.
312-455-0019

Eat: Panaderia Nuevo Leon

This self-serve Mexican bakery, operated by a father–daughter duo, has been in the community since 1973. Handmade daily, fresh favorites include vegan pink conchas pan dulce, empanadas, sweet breads, bolillos, rosca de rayes, and twelve different flavors of flour tortillas. Coming soon: a new family-owned café called **Mi Corazón Café Pilsen**.

1634 W. 18th St.
312-243-5977
www.panaderianuevoleonpilsen.com

Shop: 606 Records

The vinyl scene is alive and well in Pilsen, especially at 606 Records, which has been going strong selling new and used records since 2015. Don't be surprised if live music is happening outside the doors when you roll up. Nearby fun: **Honky Tonk BBQ**, **La Luna**, and **Throop Park**.

1808 S. Allport St.
312-585-6106
www.606records.com

Trip Planning

Choose Chicago

301 E. Cermak Rd.
312-567-8500
www.choosechicago.com

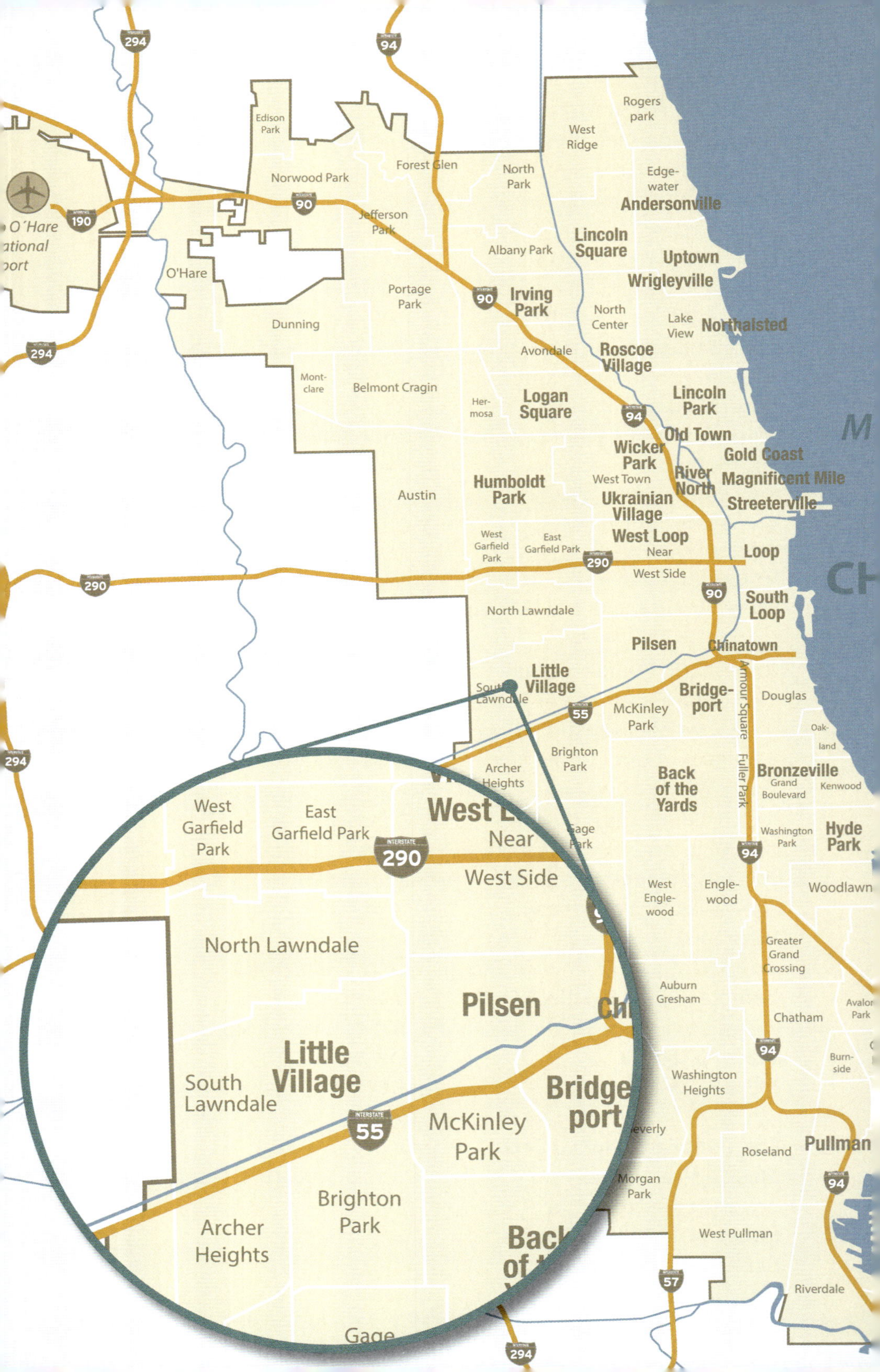

O'Hare International Airport
Edison Park
Norwood Park
Forest Glen
North Park
West Ridge
Rogers park
Edgewater
Andersonville
Jefferson Park
O'Hare
Albany Park
Lincoln Square
Uptown
Wrigleyville
Portage Park
Irving Park
North Center
Lake View
Northalsted
Dunning
Avondale
Roscoe Village
Montclare
Belmont Cragin
Hermosa
Logan Square
Lincoln Park
Old Town
Wicker Park
Gold Coast
Austin
Humboldt Park
West Town
River North
Magnificent Mile
Ukrainian Village
Streeterville
West Garfield Park
East Garfield Park
West Loop
Near West Side
Loop
South Loop
North Lawndale
Pilsen
Chinatown
Little Village
South Lawndale
Bridgeport
McKinley Park
Douglas
Armour Square
Oakland
Brighton Park
Archer Heights
Back of the Yards
Fuller Park
Bronzeville
Grand Boulevard
Kenwood
Gage Park
Washington Park
Hyde Park
West Englewood
Englewood
Woodlawn
Greater Grand Crossing
Auburn Gresham
Chatham
Avalon Park
Burnside
Washington Heights
Beverly
Roseland
Pullman
Morgan Park
West Pullman
Riverdale
294
94
190
90
290
55
57

LITTLE VILLAGE

SINCE THE 1970S, the lively enclave of Little Village, situated west of Heart of Italy and Heart of Chicago in the South Lawndale community area, has been known as "Mexico of the Midwest." This compact neighborhood, initially settled by German, Czech, and Polish immigrants, has a major commercial district—one of the largest in the city—along 26th Street. It's lovingly referred to as "La Villita" by locals, and you'll be welcomed to this vibrant area by an ornate terracotta arch that declares, "Bienvenidos a Little Village." Designed by Mexican architect Adrian Lozano and built in 1990, this arch, which was just designated a Chicago landmark in 2022, recognizes the influence of Mexican culture in Chicago.

Little Village has a plethora of annual events, including the Mexican Independence Day Parade, Villapalooza, and Little Village Posada. Spend the day eating your way through traditional bakeries, family-owned eateries, global grocery stores, food stalls, street carts, and sweet shops; viewing home-grown art in galleries and on the streets; and shopping for Mexican crafts, décor, or western wear.

Little Village Discount Mall

3115 W. 26th St. • 773-376-3700 • www.shopdiscountmall.com

✓ Dubbed the "Mexican Magnificent Mile," 26th street is one of the busiest shopping areas in not only Chicago but the entire Midwest. You'll find hundreds of mom-and-pop shops along this two-mile corridor selling everything from kid-sized mariachi ensembles to fresh mango wedges doused with chili and lime seasonings. Shops like **Artesanías Elena**, which offers crafts made by local and international Mexican artisans, and **Village Discount Outlet Store #9**, home to vintage and retro-style clothing and home goods, are highlights.

With maze-like aisles full of rainbow-colored goods, live birds, Mexican crafts, guitars, quinceañera dresses, toys, and party supplies, **Little Village Discount Mall**, situated just north of **La Villita Park**, is a sight to behold. Make sure you visit Imex Imports for traditional clothing, jewelry, and crafts for the whole family; **Chicago Pet Store**; **Antonys Western Wear** for cowboy hats and boots; and **Sophie's Shop** for wrestling masks, souvenirs, and religious figurines.

Little Village entrance (Courtesy of Powell Photography, Choose Chicago)

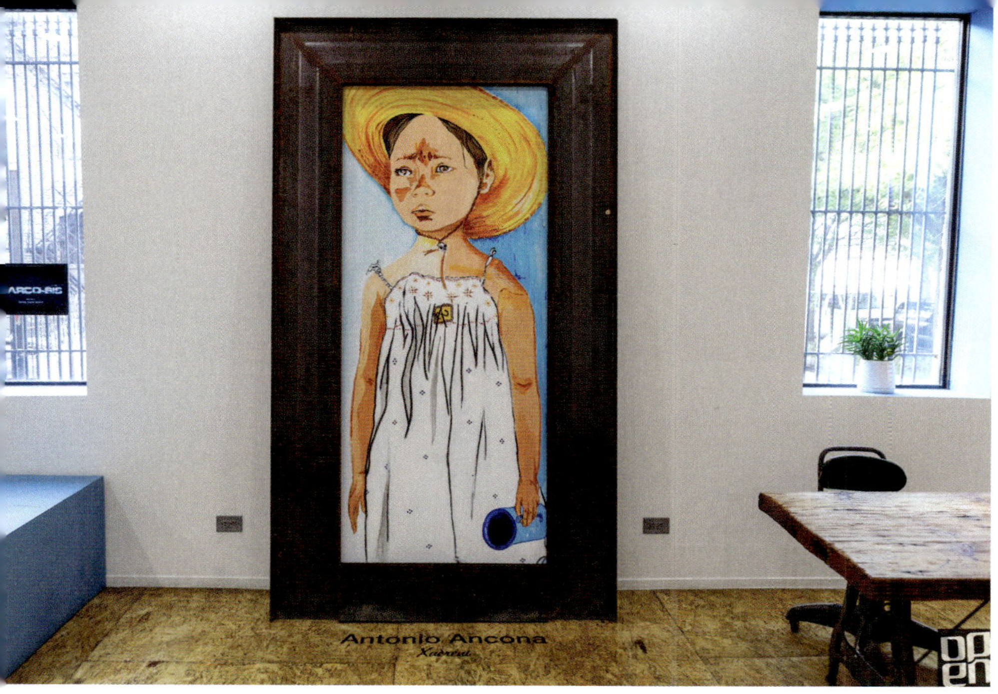

OPEN Center for the Arts (Courtesy of Carlos Aaron Magaña)

OPEN Center for the Arts

2214 S. Sacramento Ave. • 773-993-6882 • www.opencenterforthearts.org

Nothing stirs civic pride like a public gathering space for emerging and seasoned artists, educators, and entrepreneurs. OPEN, located in Marshall Square, hosts art and culture festivals, events, exhibits, and workshops meant to inspire and connect people. A fusion center and gallery, with art showcased along the building's exterior in the alley, OPEN is home to projects including Lawndale, aimed at connecting north and south Lawndale through arts programming, and Teatro Americano, an event with theater, dance, and improv. OPEN collaborates with Chicago institutions like the Lincoln Park Zoo and the **Nature Conservancy** in Illinois. Executive director and founder J. Omar Magana is an artist and impresario with a long history of supporting artists and lifting up the community. OPEN, he says on the website, is "open to all ideas and possibilities, to everyone and anyone, to all creativity in all forms, to all organizations local and international, to all the worlds. We are open."

Mi Tierra en La Villita

2528 S. Kedzie Ave. • 773-254-7722 • www.mitierraenlavillita.com

✓ The father-daughter Hispanic-owned Mi Tierra is a Little Village staple. Shareable specialties include meat, seafood, or vegetable parrilladas, served with pico de gallo, rice, and beans. And you'll delight in traditional tacos, burritos, fajitas, and enchiladas. Don't skip the dessert. Choose from churros, crepas, nieve frita, flan, or if you're really looking for a family-sized belly buster, *fuente de postres* (churros, crepes, flan, chimi-cheese, and three scoops of ice cream).

Open seven days a week for lunch and dinner, this eatery is an experience that many say is like Mexico in Chicago. Locals and visitors alike come to celebrate birthdays, anniversaries, and special events; listen to authentic Mexican mariachis as well as other live music; and enjoy a meal with family and friends on the largest patio in Little Village. The polychrome tables, chairs, and artworks match the vibrant dishes and theatrical drinks throughout the restaurant's four voluminous rooms.

Mi Tierra en La Villita (Courtesy of Powell Photography, Choose Chicago)

Nearby Alternatives

Discover: Apollo's 2000

The Art Deco Marshall Square Theater, designed by architect Alexander L. Levy, opened in 1917 for vaudeville acts and silent movies. In 1936, the theater was remodeled with a new marquee. Restored again in the '90s, the hall is now known as Apollo's 2000 and operates as an event venue for concerts, performances, and events.

2875 W. Cermak Rd.
773-247-0200
www.facebook.com/theapollos2000

Play: Manuel Perez Jr. Memorial Plaza

This petite park is the location of the annual tree lighting ceremony in December, the El Grito 5K on the morning of the Mexican Independence Day Parade, and other family-friendly events. Mosaics and colorful murals honor veteran Manuel Perez Jr., who was awarded the Congressional Medal of Honor.

26th St. and Colin Ave.
773-521-5387
www.littlevillagechamber.org

Shop: Dulcelandia del Sol

Take a trip to Candyland by visiting Dulcelandia. With over 1,000 different treats, spread out in a warehouse-style store, you can find imported sweet and spicy Mexican candies of all profiles and dimensions. Let the kids go nuts and pick out their favorites, or purchase and stuff a piñata.

3253 W. 26th St.
773-522-3816
www.dulcelandia.com

Eat: La Casa de Samuel

In addition to street food favorites, this long-standing eatery has noshes that many have never tried. House specialties include baby goat, served with pasilla sauce and cowboy beans; grilled bull's testicles, iguana, or rabbit; and slow roasted pork wrapped in a banana leaf. For dessert, order the flamed bananas cooked tableside.

2834 W. Cermak Rd.
773-376-7474
www.lacasadesamuel.com

Trip Planning

Little Village Chamber of Commerce

3610 W. 26th St.
773-521-5387
www.littlevillagechamber.org

West Loop
Near
West Side
Loop
290
90
South Loop
Lawndale
Pilsen
Chinatown
Little Village
Bridge-port
Douglas
55
McKinley Park
Armour Square
Brighton Park
Back of the Yards
Fuller Park
Bronzeville
Grand Boulevard
O´Hare
Rogers park
West Ridge
Edge-water
Andersonville
Uptown
Lake View
Northalsted
Lincoln Park
Old Town
Gold Coast
Magnificent Mile
Oak-lawn
Streeterville
Near West Side
South Lawndale
Kenwood
Archer Heights
Washington Park
Hyde Park
Garfield Ridge
West Elsdon
Gage Park
Clearing
West Lawn
Chicago Lawn
West Engle-wood
Engle-wood
Woodlawn
Greater Grand Crossing
Ashburn
Auburn Gresham
Chatham
Avalon Park
Burn-side
Washington Heights
Beverly
Mount Green-wood
Morgan Park
Roseland
Pullman
West Pullman
Riverdale
294
94
57

BRIDGEPORT

A WORKING-CLASS NEIGHBORHOOD with a culturally diverse population, Bridgeport is one of Chicago's 77 community areas, bounded by the Chicago River to north, Bubbly Creek to the west, Pershing Road to the south, and the Union Pacific railroad tracks to the east. Home of five Chicago mayors, this area boasts creative cuisine, one of Major League Baseball's oldest franchises (the Chicago White Sox), art centers and galleries, and timeless neighborhood pubs.

The skyline is dotted with historic churches and temples like First Lutheran Church of the Trinity, the oldest in Bridgeport (1865); St. Mary of Perpetual Help Catholic Church (1882); and the triangular-shaped Ling Shen Ching Tze Temple.

Several parks provide wonderful opportunities to enjoy the outdoors. The 27-acre Henry C. Palmisano Nature Park has a boardwalk, wetlands, a fishing pond, an athletic track, and lovely views. McGuane (John) Park has a sizable playground and bocce court. Park No. 571 has a boat house and launching dock for kayaking and canoeing. Armour Square Park (1905), located across from Guaranteed Rate Field, features Beaux-Arts architecture.

Chicago White Sox

333 W. 35th St. • 312-674-1000 • www.mlb.com/whitesox

☑ Major League Baseball's Chicago White Sox crack bats at Guaranteed Rate Field, where the grounds are made of bluegrass sod and dirt that was transported from the original ballpark. Crosstown rivals of the Chicago Cubs, the Sox have three World Series wins (1906, 1917, and 2005). Pick up White Sox gear at the Chicago Sports Depot and eat at ChiSox Bar & Grill, both located at Gate 5, before visiting the diamond-shaped **Champions Plaza** and the **Champions Moments** monument, outside Gate 4.

Kids love the mascot, Southpaw, a name given with a nod to the South Side as well as being a term used to describe a left-handed pitcher. Youths can join the **White Sox Kids** or **Newborn Clubs** and receive a First Game Certificate. The 15,000-square-foot Xfinity Kids Zone, open throughout the game's duration, has Sox Youth Instructors who teach baseball fundamentals like batting, pitching, and base running. Fireworks are ignited from the scoreboard after home runs.

Chicago White Sox (Courtesy of Wendy Altschuler)

Bxridgeport Art Center (Courtesy of Alberto Villegas)

Bridgeport Art Center

1200 W. 35th St. • 773-843-9000 • www.bridgeportart.com

Established in 2001, the 500,000-square-foot Bridgeport Art Center, located in the former Spiegel Catalog Warehouse, supports artists, designers, and working professionals, and has two venue spaces—the **Skyline Loft** and the **Sculpture Garden**. This imaginative space, featuring high ceilings with wood beams, exposed brick, and generous windows, is where you can see multidisciplinary art every day of the week in curated art galleries and studios.

At the **Chicago Ceramic Center** you can try your hand at pottery making. At **Wine & Paint Studio**, gather with friends and take part in an instructor-led class. **Yoga in Vogue** will help you move and relax. **Jeffrey Hirst Fine Art Studio** is where to go to learn screen printing. **Project Onward** is a gallery and studio committed to supporting artists with mental and developmental disabilities. Find unique fashion, art, and jewelry at **Gallery Row**. **Base Café** is there for you if you need to take a break.

The Duck Inn

2701 S. Eleanor St. • 312-724-8811
www.theduckinnchicago.com

☑ Surrounded by **McKinley Park**, **Pilsen**, and **Chinatown**, Bridgeport offers pretty much any type of cuisine you're looking for. And, since this dynamic neighborhood is also known as the backyard of the Chicago White Sox, there's certainly no shortage of hot dog stands and deep-dish pizza joints. For a cozy-yet-chic hot spot, hit up the retro-inspired Duck Inn, a *Michelin Guide* Bib Gourmand–designated restaurant many times over. Signature contemporary American dishes include rotisserie duck—of course—as well as an elevated Chicago-style hot dog, the Duck Inn dog, which has earned local and national accolades. Enjoy brunch or dinner inside the pre-Prohibition-era building, full of fun art and vintage nostalgia, or outside on the inviting patio. Chef, owner, and Bridgeport native Kevin Hickey, of **Four Seasons Hotel Chicago** fame, has created an enchanted space, focusing on delicious food, good-natured service, and a pleasant atmosphere.

The Duck Inn
(Courtesy of
Kevin Hartmann)

Nearby Alternatives

Discover: Zhou B Art Center

Founded in 2004, the center was created to connect local artists with a global community while promoting Eastern and Western art in the US. See a free exhibition of international and local talent, hosted by resident artists, every third Friday of the month.

1029 W. 35th St.
773-523-0200
www.zhoubartcenter.com

Discover: Chicago Maritime Museum

the Windy City began with wet feet. This museum, on the shores of Bubbly Creek inside the Bridgeport Art Center, tells the story of the city's waterways and their impact on the evolution of America. Learn about French traders, steam-powered vessels, and sailing and see the canoe collection.

1200 W. 35th St.
773-376-1982
www.chicagomaritimemuseum.org

Drink: Maria's Packaged Goods & Community Bar

Artisanal cocktails and craft beers are the specialties at this neighborhood favorite, owned and operated by two brothers and named for their mother. It's half liquor store and half tavern; you can order a beer at Maria's and mosey over to the adjoining **Kimski's**, a Polish-Korean counter-serve fusion eatery with a patio.

960 W. 31st St.
773-890-0588
www.community-bar.com

Discover: Co-Prosperity Sphere

A cultural hub and public platform for evolving art and viewpoints with exhibitions, screenings, presentations, installations, social gatherings, and performances, Co-Prosperity Sphere hosts many events each year in its 5,000-square-foot gallery space. **Public Media Institute**, a community-based art and culture organization dedicated to cultural programming, operates here.

3219 S. Morgan St.
773-823-9700
www.coprosperity.org

Trip Planning

South Loop Chamber of Commerce

1029 W. 35th St.
773-254-7225
www.southloopchamberofcommerce.com

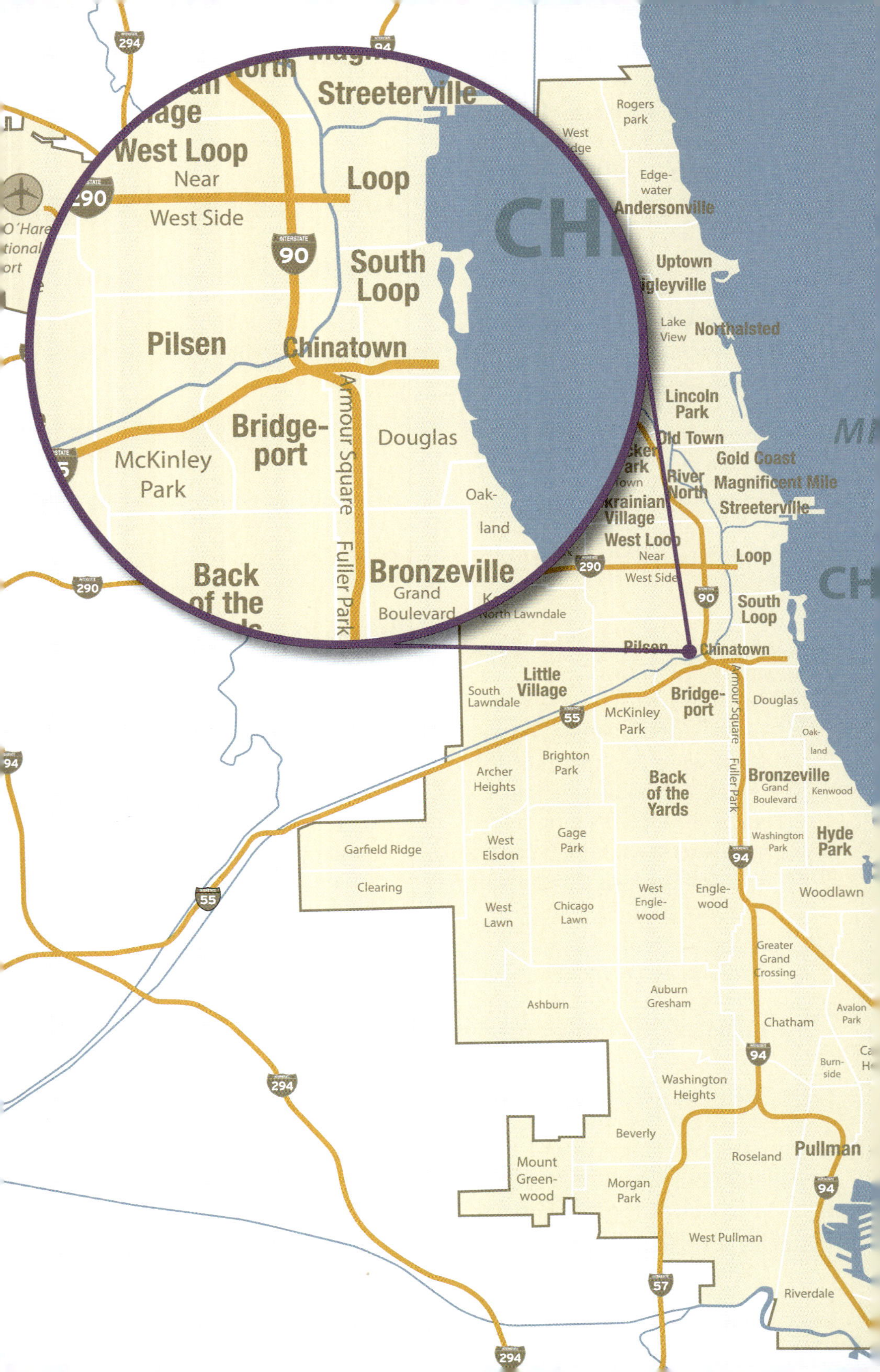
Streeterville
West Loop
Near
West Side
290
90
Loop
South
Loop
Pilsen
Chinatown
Bridge-
port
McKinley
Park
Douglas
Armour Square
Oak-
land
Fuller Park
Bronzeville
Grand
Boulevard
294
94
Rogers
park
Edge-
water
Andersonville
Uptown
Lake
View
Northalsted
Lincoln
Park
Old Town
Gold Coast
Magnificent Mile
River
North
Streeterville
West Loop
Near
West Side
Loop
South
Loop
North Lawndale
Pilsen
Chinatown
South
Lawndale
Little
Village
55
McKinley
Park
Bridge-
port
Douglas
Oak-
land
Armour Square
Fuller Park
Archer
Heights
Brighton
Park
Back
of the
Yards
Bronzeville
Grand
Boulevard
Kenwood
Garfield Ridge
West
Elsdon
Gage
Park
Washington
Park
Hyde
Park
Clearing
West
Lawn
Chicago
Lawn
West
Engle-
wood
Engle-
wood
Woodlawn
Greater
Grand
Crossing
Ashburn
Auburn
Gresham
Chatham
Avalon
Park
Burn-
side
Washington
Heights
Beverly
Mount
Green-
wood
Morgan
Park
Roseland
Pullman
West Pullman
57
Riverdale

CHINATOWN

NOT TO BE confused with Chicago's "New Chinatown," found in the West Argyle Street Historic District on the North Side, Chinatown, where over a third of the Windy City's Chinese population dwells, is burrowed on the South Side at Cermak and Wentworth Avenues. Formed in 1912, this ethnic enclave is home to vibrant specialty markets, historic architecture, and family-owned restaurants.

See the Chinatown Mural, where you can learn about the history of Chinese immigrants; stroll the Chinatown Square shopping area, ornamented with sculptures from the Chinese zodiac; and marvel at the Nine Dragon Wall. Snap photos of the Chinatown Gate, designed by Peter Fung; the firehouse where Ron Howard's film, *Backdraft*, was set; and the Chicago Public Library Chinatown Branch, which has a "living" roof, feng shui-influenced interior, and striking city views.

Part of the fun is getting there—while you could drive, the CTA Red Line is direct, and in the summer you can take a water taxi, which runs along the Chicago River from Michigan Avenue to Ping Tom Memorial Park.

Ping Tom Memorial Park

1700 S. Wentworth Ave. • 312-225-3121 • www.chicagoparkdistrict.com

Arguably one of the most picturesque parks in the city, Ping Tom Memorial Park, named after Chinatown's most celebrated civic leader, is a lovely garden-like locale with grassy knolls and Chicago River views. What was once a railroad yard is now the place to go with your family in tow for kayaking, picnicking, or romping around the children's playground.

Wander on the walking path by the water, enjoy the skyline views, and look for the **Ping Tom Pagoda**. Many special events happen here—you'd be fortunate to catch a concert, dance presentation, movie screening, or **Shakespeare in the Park** performance. See the **Stone Talk** abstract sculpture, the Ping Tom Portrait Bust, and multiple murals. Don't miss the annual **Chicago Dragon Boat Race for Literacy**, a family-friendly event starring dozens of crews, each with a drummer, that compete in eye-catching dragon boats on the south branch of the Chicago River.

Ping Tom Memorial Park (Courtesy of Adam Alexander Photography, Choose Chicago)

Street Scene, Chinese American Museum of Chicago (Courtesy of Adam Alexander Photography, Choose Chicago)

Chinese American Museum of Chicago

238 W. 23rd St. • 312-949-1000
www.ccamuseum.org

A fantastic way to learn about Chinese American culture is to visit the Chinese American Museum of Chicago. Explore temporary and permanent exhibits, take part in special educational events, watch an insightful screening, and discover how the museum tells the story of Chinese Americans in the Midwest and throughout the country.

See displays that feature emerging and professional artists; peek at ancient teapots, textiles, jewelry, paintings, photographs, and furniture; and marvel at the gorgeous "Chinese Opera" mural on the building's outdoor western wall depicting traditional Cantonese opera characters. Current exhibits include Great Wall to Great Lakes, Chinese American Veterans: Unsung Heroes, Era of Opulence: Chinese Fine Dining, and Attic Treasures II. On the second floor, listen to the stories of the people that have called Chinatown home in the short video, *My Chinatown: Stories from Within*, arranged in collaboration with the **Chicago History Museum**. Admission is free but donations are accepted.

Veggie House

2109 S. China Pl. • 312-326-9966
www.veggiehouseusa.com

✓ A treasure trove of Asian restaurants dominates Chicago's Chinatown. Whether you're interested in marinated duck, curry fish balls, fried pork intestine, shrimp dumplings, fish congee, or pork and cabbage dumplings, you won't go hungry. Located next to **Chinatown Square** sits a newfangled surprise, however.

Veggie House is the first and only exclusively vegetarian and vegan Chinese restaurant in Chinatown. This unpretentious-yet-charming eatery has a lovely little outdoor patio to match its lime-green interior. Menu items like steamed spicy dumplings, vegetable crab rangoon, Mongolian soy beef, kung pao tofu, and orange chicken nod to traditional Chinese fare. You can expect bold flavor profiles for Instagram-worthy dishes. The Taiwan noodles, inspired by a dish chef John Zhao made when he dazzled at the **Peninsula Chicago**'s famous Shanghai Terrace, are served at Veggie House for half the price. Whether you're vegetarian or vegan, or if you just appreciate a meat-free meal now and then, Veggie House won't disappoint.

Veggie House (Courtesy of Wendy Altschuler)

Nearby Alternatives

Discover: Chicago Chinese Cultural Institute

Promoting a cross-cultural understanding is the goal of Chicago Chinese Cultural Institute, where guests can learn how to make dumplings, take a tai chi class, practice their kite-making skills, or work with delicate materials during a paper cutting class. Sign up for a Chinatown walking tour, which includes the **Pui Tak Center**.

2121B South China Pl.
312-842-1988
www.chicagocci.com

Eat: Chiu Quon

Chinatown's oldest traditional Chinese bakery, Chiu Quon, offers over 100 different items, from buns to pastries, cakes, and dumplings. Choose items like barbecue pork buns, egg custard tarts, mango mousse cakes, walnut cookies, cream cones, custard buns, lotus bean mooncakes, and coconut cream turnovers. Try the house-made soy milk or milk tea.

2253 S. Wentworth Ave.
312-808-1818
www.cqbakery.com

Play: Sakura Karaoke

Billed as one of the best karaoke joints in the city, Sakura has a stage for singing, a dance floor with multicolored bright lights, two bars, and eight private VIP suites appointed with touchscreen panels, TVs, microphones, and LED lighting. Order an artisanal martini or a fun cocktail and nosh on bites.

234 W. Cermak Rd.
312-326-9168
www.sakurakaraokebar.com

Shop: AJ Housewares and Gifts

Inside this wonderfully chaotic gift shop full of lanterns, décor, incense, kitchen goods, tea sets, children's toys, and other tchotchkes is a shopping experience like no other. Afterward, wow the kids and walk a few feet to **Aji Ichiban Candy Store**, home to a large selection of Asian snacks and candy.

2125 S. China Pl.
312-567-9908

Trip Planning

Chicago Chinatown Chamber of Commerce

2169B S. China Pl.
312-326-5320
www.chicagochinatown.org

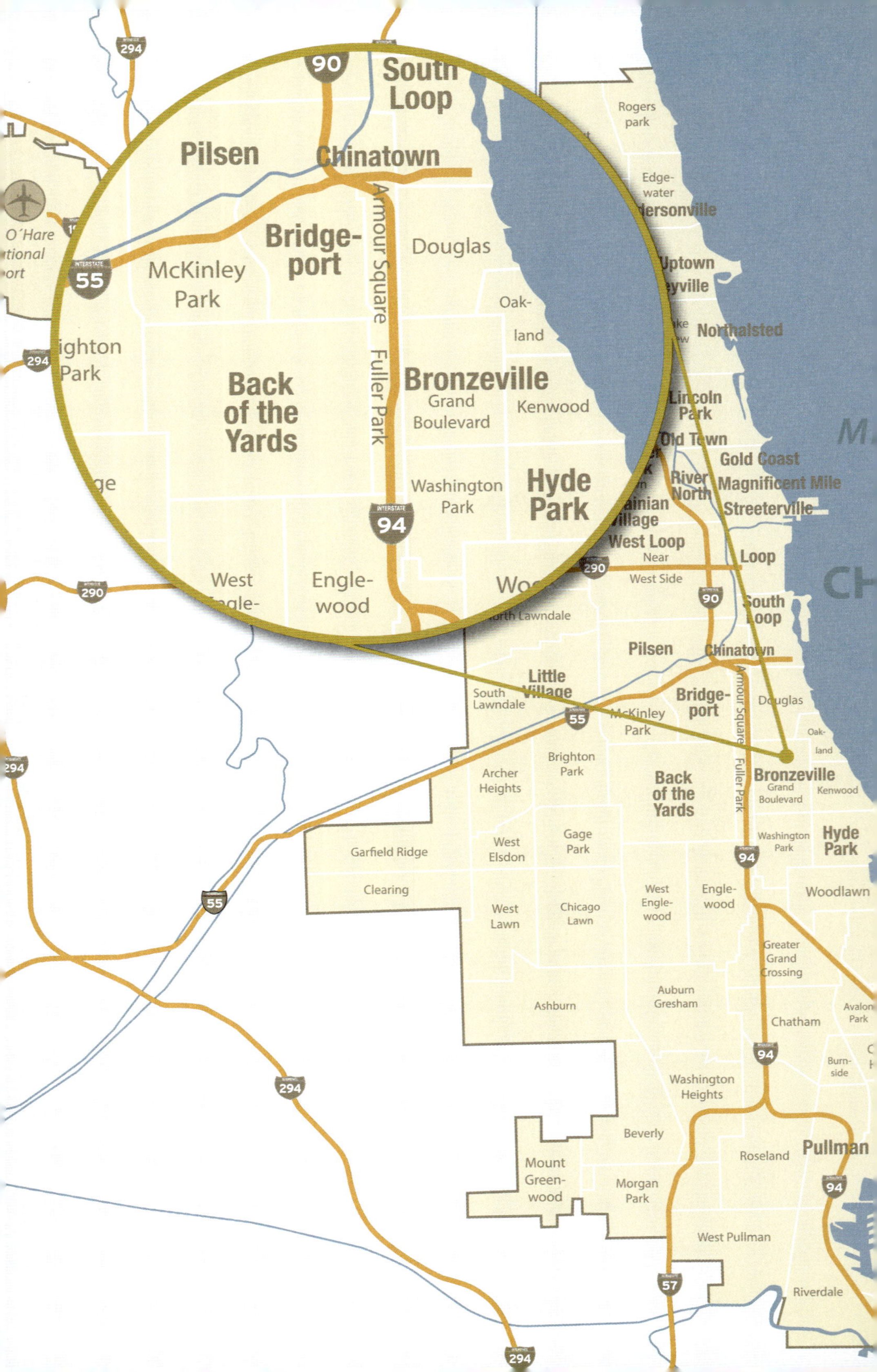

South Loop
Pilsen
Chinatown
Bridgeport
McKinley Park
Douglas
Oakland
Armour Square
Fuller Park
Back of the Yards
Bronzeville
Grand Boulevard
Kenwood
Washington Park
Hyde Park
West Englewood
Englewood
Rogers park
Edgewater
Uptown
Northalsted
Lincoln Park
Old Town
Gold Coast
Magnificent Mile
River North
Streeterville
West Loop
Near West Side
Loop
North Lawndale
Little Village
South Lawndale
Brighton Park
Archer Heights
Gage Park
West Elsdon
Garfield Ridge
Clearing
West Lawn
Chicago Lawn
Woodlawn
Greater Grand Crossing
Ashburn
Auburn Gresham
Chatham
Avalon Park
Burnside
Washington Heights
Beverly
Mount Greenwood
Morgan Park
Roseland
Pullman
West Pullman
Riverdale
O'Hare

BRONZEVILLE

THE HEART OF Chicago's African American culture beats in Bronzeville, with art, literature, music, theater, history, and vibrant events like the annual Bud Billiken Parade, our country's largest African American parade. Much like Harlem in New York City, Bronzeville, also known as the "Black Metropolis" or the "Black Belt," is bursting with soul food restaurants, coffee shops, and casual neighborhood bistros; blues, gospel, and jazz clubs; and architectural marvels and landmark structures like Unity Hall, the Forum, the Chicago Bee Building, the Chicago Defender Building, the Overton Hygienic Building, and the Supreme Life Building. Visit the Bronzeville Walk of Fame and see 92 bronze plaques from 25th Street to 35th Street. Explore the Bronzeville Art District and see the Blanc Gallery, the Bronzeville Artist Lofts, Faie Afrikan Art, Gallery Guichard, and the South Side Community Art Center.

This community, once the stomping grounds of the Marx Brothers, Gwendolyn Brooks, Ida B. Wells, Bessie Coleman, Jesse Owens, Nat "King" Cole, Sam Cooke, and Louis Armstrong, has an energy that makes it one of the most remarkable in the Windy City.

Harold Washington Cultural Center

4701 S. Martin Luther King Jr. Dr. • 773-373-1900
www.broadwayinbronzeville.com

☑ Harold Washington, a native Chicagoan and graduate of Roosevelt and Northwestern Universities, served 16 years in the state legislature and two years in the House before he was elected mayor in 1983. The Harold Washington Cultural Center, located at historic 47th St. and Dr. Martin Luther King Drive, was once the site of the **Regal Theater**, where Duke Ellington played. This 42,000-square-foot nonprofit performing arts and education facility has a 1,000-seat theater, video editing lab, full-service recording studio, dance and tap studios, computer lab, exhibition hall, and museum. Over 25,000 young students participate in programs each year.

With a commitment to children, culture, and community, the Harold Washington Cultural Center works with Broadway in **Bronzeville Productions**, the in-house production company that serves the community through the arts in keeping with its motto, "Off the streets and on the stage."

Harold Washington Cultural Center
(Courtesy of Powell Photography, Choose Chicago)

Home to Bronzeville Children's Museum (Courtesy of Powell Photography, Choose Chicago)

Bronzeville Children's Museum

9301 S. Stony Island Ave. • 773-721-9301
www.bronzevillechildrensmuseum.com

✓ Operating as the first and only African American children's museum in the country, this nonprofit institution, founded in 1993, is an important part of the community, especially for kids between the ages of four and nine.

Children can learn about African American inventors like Lewis H. Latimer, who invented carbon filaments for light bulbs, and Garrett A. Morgan, who invented the traffic light on the African American Inventors tour; explore the world of STEM (Science, Technology, Engineering, and Math); and take guided tours of famous Bronzeville landmarks. Key educational messages are communicated to each child throughout the displays. There's an immersive, hands-on veterinarian exhibit; the play *Jewel Store*; a healthy eating exhibit called You Are What You Eat; a play, *Provident Hospital*, honoring the first African American hospital in the country; and plenty of annual events and activities to celebrate African American culture and history. Admission is only $5.

Pearl's Place

3901 S. Michigan Ave. • 773-285-1700
www.pearlsplacerestaurant.com

✓ African Americans journeyed to Bronzeville during the Great Migration. See Alison Saar's bronze *Monument to the Great Northern Migration*, honoring the many people who trekked to Chicago from the South in the early 20th century in search of liberty and opportunity. Travel to **Dunbar Park**, a 22-acre community space featuring a playground, reading garden, and sculpture of Paul Laurence Dunbar, one of the first African American poets to gain success. Visit **Olivet Baptist Church**, the second-oldest African American church in the city.

Make your way to Pearl's Place, a long-standing, popular restaurant, serving delectable Southern-style soul food. Order shrimp and cheese grits or catfish nuggets for an appetizer, jambalaya for dinner, and peach cobbler for dessert, or fill up your plate at the breakfast, lunch, or dinner buffet. Wear your stretchy pants for the belly-busting delights at this classic white-tablecloth elevated neighborhood eatery, perfect for bringing your whole family.

Pearl's Place (Courtesy of Abel Arciniega, @tequilagraphics, Choose Chicago)

Nearby Alternatives

Discover: Illinois Institute of Technology

Meet inside Perlstein Hall for a tour with the Chicago Architecture Center and see a collection of buildings designed by Ludwig Mies van der Rohe, one of the most influential figures to shape the Chicago skyline. The tour spotlights the period the architect was the head of the School of Architecture, from 1939 to 1958.

10 W. 33rd St.
312-922-3432
www.architecture.org

Discover: Gallery Guichard

On the first floor of the historic Bronzeville Artist Lofts (1906), originally Borden's Dairy, Gallery Guichard showcases a collection of modern and contemporary art from multicultural global artists, specializing in the art of the African Diaspora. Proudly nestled in the largest African American art district in America, this gallery is a must-see.

436 E. 47th St.
773-791-7003
www.galleryguichard.com

Play: 31st Street Beach

31st Street Beach, known as Margaret T. Burroughs Beach, is located south of **McCormick Place Bird Sanctuary** and north of **Burnham Skate Park**. Enjoy skyline views, a playground, a fishing dock, and a harbor for small boats. Steps from the sand is **Pier 31 Restaurant** with a deck.

3100 S. Jean-Baptiste Pointe DuSable Lake Shore Dr.
312-74-BEACH
www.chicagoparkdistrict.com

Discover: Robert W. Roloson Houses

See the only Frank Lloyd Wright row homes ever built, which anchor the Gap community. Designed in 1894 and completed in 1895, they're listed on the National Register of Historic Places and designated a Chicago Landmark. While you can't go inside, you can visit the Art Institute of Chicago to see balusters.

3213–3219 S. Calumet Ave.
312-443-3600
www.artic.edu

Trip Planning

Bronzeville Chamber of Commerce

710 E. 47th St.
773-268-1800
www.bronzevillechamber.com

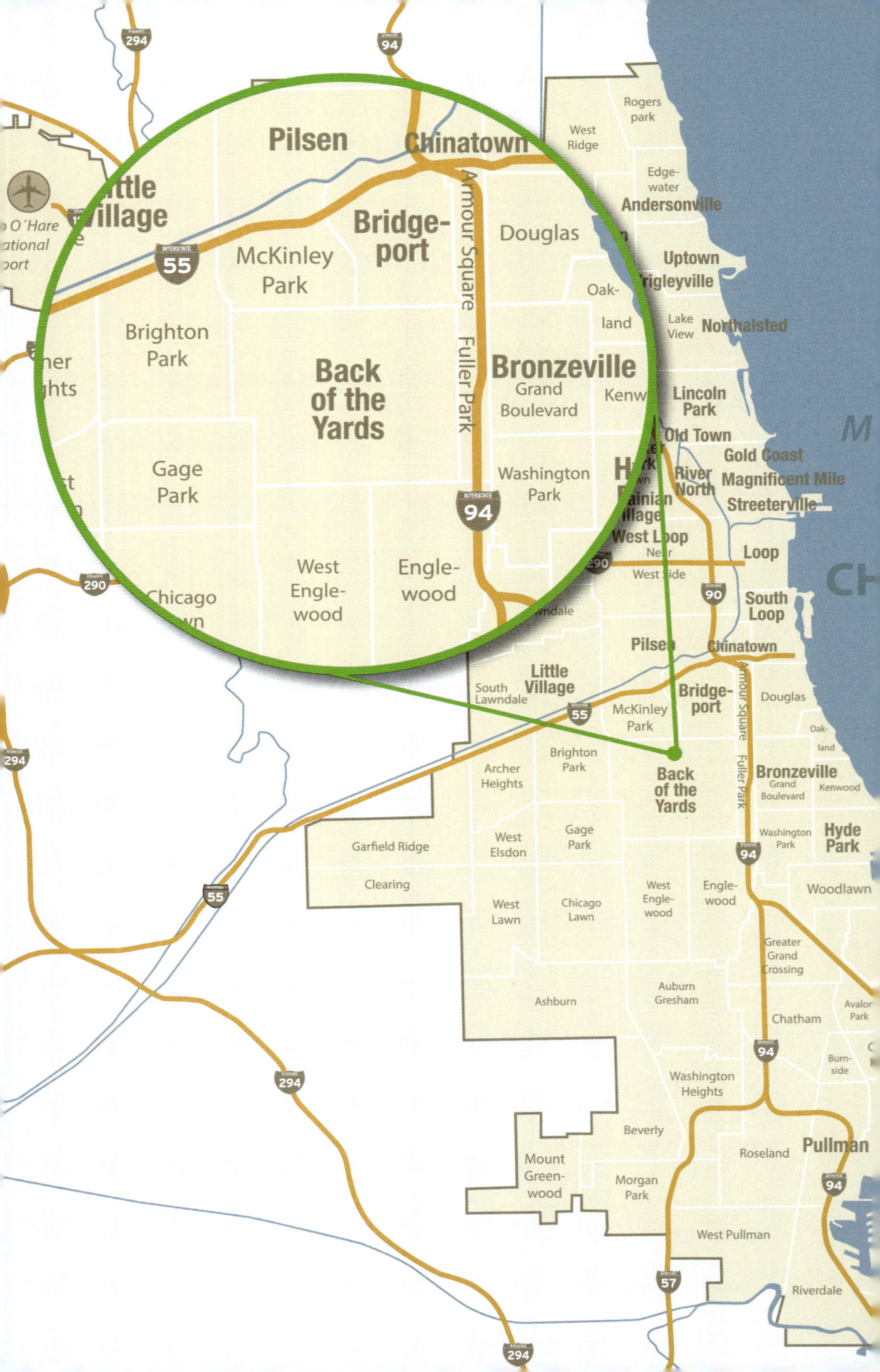

Pilsen
Chinatown
Little Village
Bridgeport
Armour Square
Douglas
McKinley Park
Oakland
Brighton Park
Back of the Yards
Fuller Park
Bronzeville
Grand Boulevard
Gage Park
Washington Park
West Englewood
Englewood
Chicago Lawn
Rogers park
West Ridge
Edgewater
Andersonville
Uptown
Lake View
Northalsted
Lincoln Park
Old Town
Gold Coast
Magnificent Mile
River North
Streeterville
West Loop
Near West Side
Loop
South Loop
South Lawndale
Archer Heights
Kenwood
Hyde Park
Garfield Ridge
West Elsdon
Clearing
West Lawn
Woodlawn
Greater Grand Crossing
Ashburn
Auburn Gresham
Chatham
Avalon Park
Burnside
Washington Heights
Beverly
Mount Greenwood
Morgan Park
Roseland
Pullman
West Pullman
Riverdale

BACK OF THE YARDS

PART OF THE New City Community Area, Back of the Yards is immortalized in Upton Sinclair's *The Jungle*. It's situated in the South Side district, where Lithuanian, Czech, Polish, Irish, and German immigrants originally settled here for work. The notorious Union Stock Yards, which made Chicago the "hog butcher for the world," was a massive meatpacking district in operation from 1865 to 1971.

What remains today is the beautiful limestone Union Stock Yard Gate, a designated Chicago Landmark and National Historic Landmark, situated next to the firefighters' memorial. Long-standing businesses thrive here, including Taqueria Atotonilco, known for its fresh tacos prepared with Illinois-grown corn tortillas made in its neighboring factory and chocolate and strawberry licuados. From well-attended swap markets to coffee roasters and shops—Sputnik Coffee Company and Back of the Yards Coffee House are the top—to Davis Square and Sherman Parks to bakeries like El Original Acambaro Bakery, Bake for Me!, and Just Cakes Bakery to breweries—Whiner Beer Co. and Marz Community Brewing Company, this neighborhood has a strong community vibe, full of hard workers who stick together.

The Plant

1400 W. 46th St. • 773-357-7192
www.insidetheplant.com

✓ The Plant, a unique research and production operation owned and operated by Bubbly Dynamics, does much for the community. What was once the industrial Peer Foods meatpacking plant is now a 100,000-square-foot, eco-friendly laboratory and incubator for over 20 food and farming small businesses. Nearly 100 employees work in-house at diverse businesses like **Arize Kombucha**, **Kombuchade**, **Whiner Beer Co.**, **Bike a Bee**, **CacaoAbunga**, **Closed Loop Farms**, **Sacred Serve**, **Four Letter Word Coffee**, and **Great American Cheese Collection**—and the Plant is still growing.

The main ethos of the Plant is to create a collaborative society where earth-friendly best practices close the loops of waste and energy for food- and beverage-producing trades. Check out the calendar of events and support resident companies by visiting the Plant's **Whiner Beer Co.** taproom or **Turtle Stop** retail shop, where you can find the Plant products; see the **Packingtown Museum**; and take a tour of the Plant.

The Plant (Courtesy of Bubbly Dynamics LLC)

Sherman Park (Courtesy of Wendy Altschuler)

Sherman Park

1301 W. 52nd St. • 312-747-6672
www.chicagoparkdistrict.com

Opened in 1905, Sherman Park was named after John B. Sherman, Daniel Burnham's father-in-law and a founder of **Chicago's Union Stock Yards**. Renowned landscape architects and brothers John Charles and Frederick Law Olmsted, along with Daniel H. Burnham, designed the park to improve the lives of the immigrant and working-class population in the surrounding neighborhood.

With a distinctive, winding waterway that circles an island of ballfields, this park is a lovely place to spend the afternoon. On the north end of the park, see the classically designed field house and gym, complete with pergolas. Relish fresh air and exercise—you'll find a swimming pool, basketball court, indoor gym, baseball diamonds, soccer field, auditorium, tennis courts, and multiple playgrounds. This nearly 60-acre green space is home to several seasonal events and programs like the senior sock hop dance, jazz concerts, and festive, holiday-themed parties.

Stanley's

4258 S. Ashland Ave. • 773-927-0033
www.facebook.com/stanleysashland

✔ A tavern-filled boozy zone known as Whiskey Row is where workers would go after a long day in the stockyards. In 1924, Stanley Kurek opened his first tavern on Ashland Avenue, and in 1935, he built the current two-story tavern that he ran until his death in 1957. Stanley's son Ted ran it until he died in 1983, at which point Stanley's daughter Wanda Kurek stepped up until she died at the age of 95 in 2019 (Wanda lived above the bar).

Stanley's is the only **Whiskey Row** tavern left, and it continues to serve lunch on weekdays with always-changing menu specialties like soups, burgers, sandwiches, meatloaf, pork chops, Italian sausage, baked ham with yams, and hot turkey. Eat while listening to music squeaking out of a vintage jukebox. This gem has little to no online presence—most folks who frequent Stanley's are on a first-name basis with everyone inside.

Stanley's (Courtesy of Wendy Altschuler)

Nearby Alternatives

Drink: Marz Community Brewing Company

Marz, which opened in 2013, is located across Bubbly Creek in McKinley Park's Central Manufacturing District. Here you can sip one of two dozen beers on draft at the art-filled taproom, complete with an oval-shaped bar. Pizza from **East Free Pizza** and desserts from **Bittersweet Bakery** will satisfy any cravings.

3630 S. Iron St.
773-579-1935
www.marz.beer

Play: Razzmatazz

Fun for the whole family, Razzmatazz Game & Grill is a large arcade with a variety of immersive video games and food options like pizza, wings, sandwiches, burgers, and churros. Kids can bowl, jump on the inflatable playground, earn prizes, and join family and friends for birthday celebrations.

3900 S. Ashland Ave.
773-762-3380
www.razzmatazzchicago.com

Drink: Back of the Yards Coffee House

This small business is determined to benefit the neighborhood by honoring its working class as well as its immigrant-powered past through its SEED (social impact, economic development, environmental responsibility, direct relations) mission. Resilient and robust not only defines their beans, but also their philosophy.

2059 W. 47th St.
773-475-6381
www.backoftheyardscoffee.com

Shop: Swap-O-Rama Flea Market

Wear your comfy shoes and prepare for an afternoon of shopping at this market, home to an average of 500 sellers inside and 600 sellers outside. Swap-O-Rama opened "the granddaddy of all flea markets" on Ashland Avenue in 1992, and currently over 20,000 shoppers wander through each weekend.

4100 S. Ashland Ave.
708-344-7300
www.swap-o-rama.com

Trip Planning

Back of the Yards Neighborhood Council

1823 W. 47th St.
872-281-7832
www.bync.org

Douglas
Oak-
land
Bronzeville
Grand
Boulevard
Kenwood
Fuller Park
Washington
Park
Hyde
Park
94
Engle-
wood
Woodlawn
Greater
Grand
Crossing
South
Shore
Avalon
Rogers
park
LAKE
MICHIG
CHICAG
Streeterville
Loop
90
South
Loop
Pilsen
Chinatown
Little
Village
South
Lawndale
Bridge-
port
McKinley
Park
55
Armour Square
Brighton
Park
Archer
Heights
Back
of the
Yards
Garfield Ridge
West
Elsdon
Gage
Park
Clearing
West
Lawn
Chicago
Lawn
West
Engle-
wood
Auburn
Gresham
Ashburn
Chatham
Avalon
Park
South
Chicago
Burn-
side
Calumet
Heights
Washington
Heights
Beverly
Roseland
Pullman
South
Deering
Mount
Green-
wood
Morgan
Park
West Pullman
57
Riverdale
Hegew
294

HYDE PARK

SANDWICHED BETWEEN WASHINGTON and Jackson Parks, connected by the one-mile-long Midway Plaisance that flows through the University of Chicago campus, Hyde Park is an urban dream. One of the city's Community Areas, located on the South Side, it affords easy access to the Museum of Science and Industry, housed in the former Palace of Fine Arts from the 1893 World's Columbian Exposition; Frank Lloyd Wright's Robie House; Promontory Point, a peninsula that stretches out into Lake Michigan; and the 57th and 63rd Street Beaches.

Hyde Park was the stomping grounds of many famous folks—Muhammad Ali, Amelia Earhart, Marshall Field, Hugh Hefner, and Harold Washington. President Barack Obama was a senior lecturer for 12 years at the University of Chicago Law School, and now the Obama Presidential Center is under construction.

Shopping and dining abound, especially at 53rd Street, the neighborhood's oldest retail district, complete with farmers market; 55th Street, where you can enjoy global cuisine; and 57th Street, home to independent bookshops and the 57th Street Art Fair, Chicago's oldest juried art fair.

JACKSON PARK

6401 S. Stony Island Ave. • 773-256-0903 • www.chicagoparkdistrict.com

It's easy to whittle away the day exploring Jackson Park's 552 acres, stretching from **Hyde Park** to **Woodlawn** along Lake Michigan. The **Museum of Science and Industry** at the north end of the park is a good place to start. Next, soak up the sun at 57th Street Beach, accessible via a pedestrian underpass, featuring a distance swimming area. Make your way to the **Japanese Garden**, also called Garden of the Phoenix or Osaka Garden, located on the park's **Wooden Island**, and see the pavilion, moon bridge, Osaka Gate, blossoming cherry trees, and Yoko Ono's Sky Landing sculpture, all standing on the site of the 1893 World's Columbian Exposition's Japanese Pavilion.

Nearby, across the East Lagoon, sits **Bobolink Meadow**, **Jackson Bark** dog park and **Jackson Park Driving Range**. Farther south, you'll find the **63rd Street Beach**, home to the city's oldest beach house, with 12 acres of native dune habitat.

Jackson Park (Courtesy of Powell Photography, Choose Chicago)

Museum of Science and Industry (Courtesy of Heidi Peters, Museum of Science and Industry, Chicago)

Museum of Science and Industry

5700 S. DuSable Lake Shore Dr.
773-684-1414 • www.msichicago.org

✔ Easily one of the city's largest and best museums, with hundreds of exhibits, the Museum of Science and Industry is a must on any Chicago itinerary. Visit the museum's very first exhibit, Coal Mine, which takes you on an interactive, guided, underground adventure that teaches you about mining methods and machinery. Dissect a cow eyeball with a scalpel in the lab, see the *Pioneer Zephyr*, board the U-505 submarine, check out a flight and motion simulator, and watch real chicks hatch. Observe scientists drop objects off a 25-foot balcony to show elastic energy transforming into motion energy, learn about storms, and watch lighting (indoors!) via the Tesla Coil. Be sure to see the Fairy Castle, Ships Gallery, Mirror Maze, Idea Factory, and domed five-story movie theater.

Don't be surprised if your kids become budding scientists or engineers after experiencing MSI's interactive exhibits, scientist-led activities, and engaging film screenings.

Valois Restaurant

1518 E. 53rd St. • 773-667-0647 • www.valoisrestaurant.com

✓ Treat yourself to a tour of Obama's Chicago by first stopping at their South Side home located in the Kenwood neighborhood at 5046 S. Greenwood Ave. Wander past the **Hyde Park Hair Salon**, Obama's barber of 20 years; visit **Burnham Park**, with Instagram-worthy views of Chicago's skyline; and see the **Obama Kissing Rock**, the adorable site of the couple's first kiss, located at 53rd and South Dorchester. There's a plaque, attached to a boulder, that reads, "On our first date, I treated her to the finest ice cream **Baskin-Robbins** had to offer, our dinner table doubling as the curb. I kissed her, and it tasted like chocolate."

Finally, you'll want to eat at Valois Restaurant, Barack Obama's favorite cafeteria-style breakfast and lunch spot, where you can "see your food." One of the oldest of its kind in the country, established in 1921, Valois serves large, wholesome meals to loyal diners.

Valois Restaurant (Courtesy of Rachel Bires, Choose Chicago)

Nearby Alternatives

Discover: Obama Presidential Center

Ground broke on this museum and gathering space, named after the nation's first African American President and First Lady. With an auditorium, broadcast and recording studios, restaurant, library, activity center, kids' area, and gardens, it will be a place that honors history, inspires youth, and creates economic prosperity.

Jackson Park

www.obama.org/the-center

Discover: Frederick C. Robie House

Tour the Prairie-style Robie House, completed in 1910 by maverick architect Frank Lloyd Wright. A National Historic Landmark, the three-story marvel sits near the University of Chicago and is designed with a horizontal composition and cantilevered rooflines. UNESCO designated the house, along with seven other Wright buildings, as World Heritage sites.

5757 S. Woodlawn Ave.

312-994-4000

www.franklloydwright.org

Discover: Oriental Institute Museum

One of the world's first interdisciplinary institutes, The University of Chicago's **Oriental Institute**, founded by James Henry Breasted in 1919, has 350,000 artifacts. Most were excavated by Oriental Institute archaeologists, and 5,000 of them are on display. This leading research center is home to galleries dedicated to the earliest civilizations.

1155 E. 58th Ave.

773-702-9514

www.oi100.uchicago.edu

Discover: The DuSable Black History Museum and Education Center

The nation's first and oldest independent Black history and education museum, named after Chicago's first permanent settler, Jean Baptiste Point du Sable, has more than 15,000 paintings, sculptures, print works, and memorabilia items. See the exhibits and take part in insightful workshops, lectures, or online events that highlight historical achievements of African Americans.

740 E. 56th PL.

773-947-0600

www.dusablemuseum.org

Trip Planning

Hyde Park Chamber of Commerce

1525 E. 53rd St.

773-288-0124

www.hydeparkchamberchicago.org

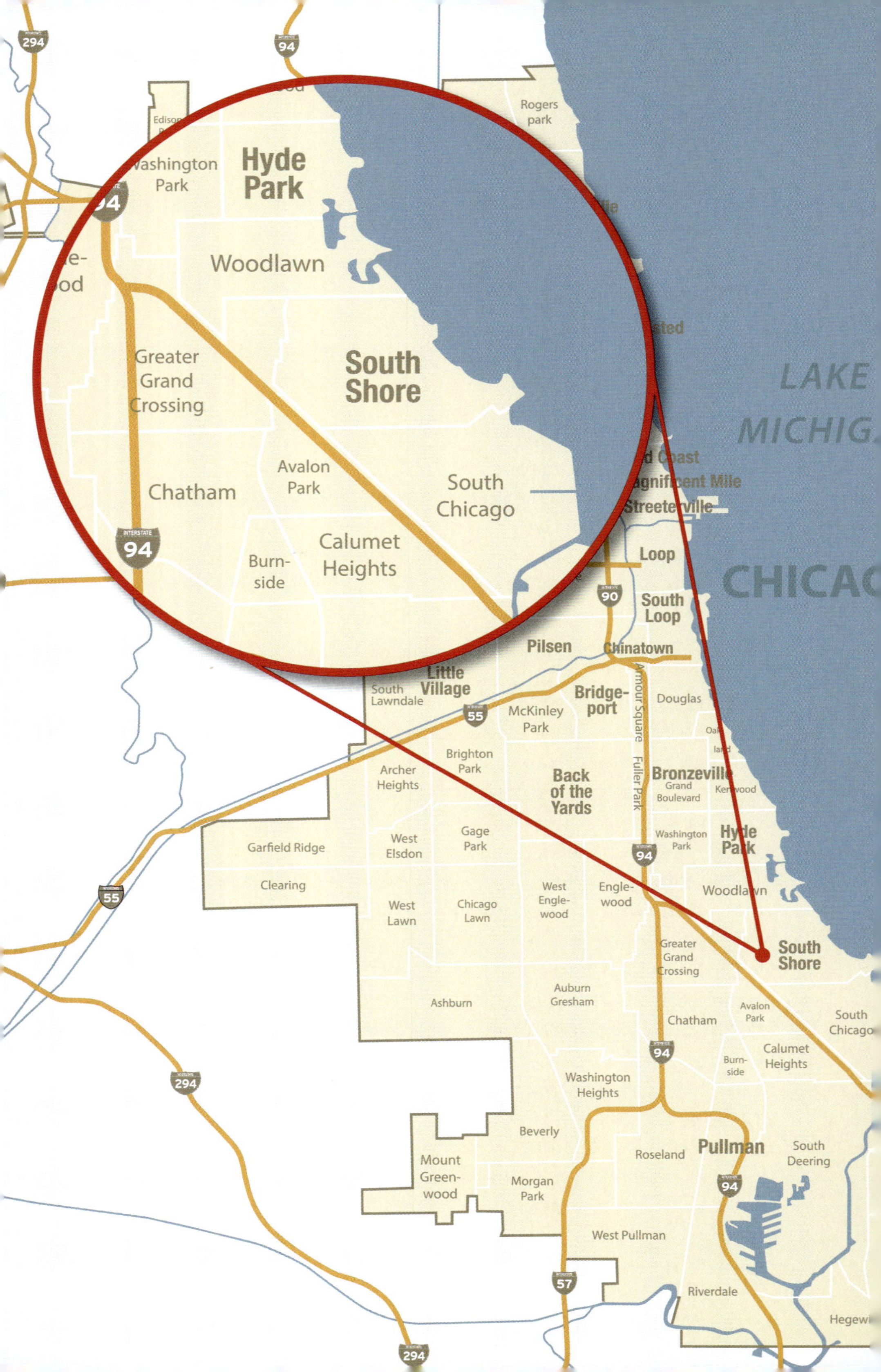

Hyde Park
Washington Park
Woodlawn
South Shore
Greater Grand Crossing
Chatham
Avalon Park
South Chicago
Calumet Heights
Burn-side
LAKE MICHIGAN
CHICAGO
Rogers park
Streeterville
Loop
South Loop
Pilsen
Chinatown
Little Village
South Lawndale
Bridge-port
McKinley Park
Douglas
Brighton Park
Archer Heights
Back of the Yards
Bronzeville
Grand Boulevard
Kenwood
Armour Square
Fuller Park
Garfield Ridge
Clearing
West Elsdon
Gage Park
Washington Park
West Lawn
Chicago Lawn
West Engle-wood
Engle-wood
Ashburn
Auburn Gresham
Washington Heights
Beverly
Mount Green-wood
Morgan Park
Roseland
Pullman
South Deering
West Pullman
Riverdale
294
94
90
55
57

SOUTH SHORE

ONE OF THE White City's defined Community Areas located along the waterfront, South Shore was once a fast-growing neighborhood due to its proximity to the 1893 World's Columbian Exposition, a social and cultural world's fair held in Chicago's Jackson Park to celebrate the 400th anniversary of Christopher Columbus's arrival in the New World. The first established community within South Shore, where elegant homes with sizable, manicured lawns dominated the landscape, was Jackson Park Highlands, established in 1905.

Beyond exploring historic districts, residents and locals today enjoy the capacious lakefront, with one of the largest beaches in the city; diverse dining and coffee options, like Chef Sarah's Café or South Shore Brew; a plethora of cultural activities; and outdoor fun like the South Shore Nature Sanctuary, where you'll find a microcosm of native Illinois natural habitats within the South Shore Cultural Center Park. Notably, First Lady Michelle Obama grew up in South Shore in a Chicago bungalow located at 7436 S. Euclid Avenue, a house that was built in the 1920s not far from Rosenblum Park.

South Shore Cultural Center

7059 S. South Shore Dr. • 773-256-0149 • www.chicagoparkdistrict.com

✔ Featured in *The Blues Brothers* and the site of Barack and Michelle Obama's wedding reception, the South Shore Cultural Center is a prominent Chicago Landmark building listed on the National Register of Historic Places. Formerly the exclusive **South Shore Country Club**, founded in 1905 and rebuilt in 1916, the original structure was designed in a Mediterranean Revival style and the grounds included a clubhouse, stables, golf and tennis courts, a bowling green, and a private beach on Lake Michigan. In 1975, the **Chicago Park District** took over the building and renamed it the South Shore Cultural Center.

See the solarium, formal dining hall, art gallery, and **Paul Robeson Theatre** on the interior. Then explore the grounds, where you'll find a formal garden, golf course, beach, nature sanctuary, and butterfly garden. Discover a plethora of cultural programs and classes for all ages, including dance, music, art, fitness, and cooking.

South Shore Cultural Center (Courtesy of Wendy Altschuler)

Rainbow Beach and Park (Courtesy of Wendy Altschuler)

Rainbow Beach and Park

3111 E. 77th St. • 312-745-1479 • www.chicagoparkdistrict.com

☑ Spend the day at Rainbow Beach and the surrounding Rainbow Beach Park, which offers stunning Lake Michigan and skyline views. Named for the **US Army's 42nd Rainbow Division** that battled in World War I, Rainbow Beach features a gym, fitness center, several sports courts, and distance swimming. The **Chicago Park District** built a field house in 1999, designed by David Woodhouse Architects. Children can play at the **Rainbow Beach Playground**. Be sure to visit the dune habitat and see the granite monument commemorating the 50th Anniversary of the Rainbow Division of WWII, constructed by veterans in 1967. Special happenings include kids' clubs, movie nights, and holiday events.

Rainbow Beach Victory Garden is not only one of the largest and oldest historic beachside community gardens in the city, full of vegetables and flowers, but also one of the last victory gardens left—during World War II there were around 20 million.

Surf's Up South Shore

2236 East 71st St. • 773-891-5544 • www.surfsupchi.com

✓ History buffs will be interested in the 16-square-block community of **Jackson Park Highlands**, a designated Chicago Landmark district where most of the homes were built between 1905 and 1940. This planned model community has landscaped lots with brick or stone houses set back from the property line. Architectural styles include American Four Square, Classical Revival, Queen Anne, Dutch Colonial, Colonial Revival, Tudor, Prairie School, and Craftsman. Notable residents have included former Chicago Bears player Gale Sayers, blues legend Bo Diddley, and Jesse Jackson.

After seeing the historic district, make your way to nearby Surf's Up South Shore, a casual Cajun and seafood gem where Hennessy wings are served every day. Favorites include shrimp and cheese grits, fried green tomatoes, and thick po' boy sandwiches. Owned by Vanetta D. Roy, a special education teacher for Chicago public schools, Surf's Up is committed to shining a positive light on the South Shore community.

Surf's Up (Courtesy of Wendy Altschuler)

Nearby Alternatives

Discover: Stony Island Arts Bank

What was once the neoclassical Stony Island Trust and Savings Bank during most of the twenties is now an art gallery, media archive, library, and community center listed on the National Register of Historic Places. Transformed by the Rebuild Foundation, founded by Theaster Gates, it's now a spot where the community comes together through art, film, and music.

6760 S. Stony Island Ave.
312-857-5561
www.rebuild-foundation.org

Play: Rainbow Beach Dunes Natural Area

See one of the most ecologically important natural areas with native plants along the lakefront at Rainbow Beach Dunes, a beach, wetland, and dune habitat where over 250 migrating bird species have been documented. The area is managed by the park district, and a stewardship program is in place with ongoing restoration projects.

3111 E. 77th St.
312-74-BEACH
www.chicagoparkdistrict.com

Eat: Majani Soulful Vegan

This Black-owned business serves up flavorful Southern cuisine with a twist—it's vegan. From fried grits and okra to tacos, bowls, salads, burgers, and wraps, you can find innovative delights made with wholesome ingredients any time of year. Don't skip dessert—cookies or chocolate, lemon, strawberry, or carrot cupcakes.

7167 S. Exchange Ave.
773-359-4019
www.majani.biz

Discover: eta Creative Arts Foundation

A central arts and education institution since 1971, highlighting Black culture through theater, eta provides training and performance opportunities for youth and adults. See live theater and hear a range of musical styles in the 200-seat theater and visit the library, community room, art gallery, and workshop.

7558 S. South Chicago Ave.
773-752-3955
www.etacreativearts.org

Trip Planning

South Shore Chamber of Commerce

21750 E. 71st St.
773-955-9508
www.southshorechamberinc.org

LAKE
MICHIGA
CHICAG
Chatham
Avalon Park
Calumet Heights
Burn-side
Washington Heights
Pullman
Roseland
South Deering
West Pullman
Riverdale
Rogers park
Gold Coast
Magnificent Mile
Streeterville
Loop
South Loop
Pilsen
Chinatown
Little Village
South Lawndale
Bridge-port
McKinley Park
Douglas
Oak-land
Armour Square
Fuller Park
Brighton Park
Archer Heights
Back of the Yards
Bronzeville
Grand Boulevard
Kenwood
Washington Park
Hyde Park
Garfield Ridge
West Elsdon
Gage Park
Clearing
West Lawn
Chicago Lawn
West Engle-wood
Engle-wood
Woodlawn
Greater Grand Crossing
South Shore
Ashburn
Auburn Gresham
Chatham
Avalon Park
South Chicago
Calumet Heights
Burn-side
Washington Heights
Beverly
Roseland
Pullman
South Deering
Mount Green-wood
Morgan Park
West Pullman
Riverdale
Hegewisch
294
94
90
55
57

PULLMAN

RAILWAY MAGNATE AND wealthy industrialist George Pullman is well known not only for his Pullman Palace Car Company, but also for the amenity-filled community he built for his workers. Designated by President Barack Obama in 2015, the Pullman National Historical Park, also called the Pullman District, is the first National Park Service unit in the City of Big Shoulders. Learn the story about one of the first planned industrial towns in America, its role in American labor history with the 1894 Pullman Strike, and its impact on urban planning, design, and architecture.

Visitors to the Pullman National Historical Park will see the Historic Pullman Foundation Pullman Exhibit Hall; Hotel Florence, named after Pullman's firstborn child; the Administration Clock Tower Building; the National A. Philip Randolph Pullman Porter Museum, which honors African American labor history; Historic Pullman Workers' Homes, built in the original 1880's Pullman Company Town; Greenstone Church, currently named Greenstone United Methodist Church; the Historic Pullman Wheelworks; the Pullman Firehouse; Market Hall; and Arcade Park. Explore the quarter on your own or take a guided tour for an in-depth experience.

Clock Tower Administration Building

610 E. 111th St. • 773-468-9310
www.nps.gov

The best place to begin your tour of historic Pullman is at the elaborate Clock Tower Administration Building, built in 1880, which is home to the new **Pullman Visitor Center**. Exhibits and programs are offered here, telling the stories surrounding George Pullman's company and vision, labor rights, manufacturing, and urban planning. Located just north of **Exhibit Hall**, where you'll find more artifacts and informative exhibits from the **Historic Pullman Foundation**'s collection, you can also talk to a park ranger and pick up an informative brochure to help you navigate on your own around the district. Seasonal guided walking tours are also available on the first Sunday of the month.

Kids can become a Pullman junior ranger, earning an official Pullman junior ranger badge, by completing activities in a national park service booklet during their visit, sharing their answers with a park ranger, and taking a pledge to protect our parks.

Pullman exhibit (Courtesy of Powell Photography, Choose Chicago)

Pullman exhibit (Courtesy of Powell Photography, Choose Chicago)

Philip Randolph Pullman Porter Museum

10406 S. Maryland Ave. • 773-850-8580 • www.aprpullmanportermuseum.org

Pullman National Historical Park, which became part of the African American Civil Rights Network in 2019, commemorates the breakthrough unionization of African American workers with the Brotherhood of Sleeping Car Porters (BSCP), founded by Asa Philip Randolph in 1925. **Pullman Palace Car Company** was the country's largest employer of African Americans when a major labor agreement, made between Pullman and the first African American labor union in the country recognized by the American Federation of Labor, was reached in 1937.

Beyond labor organizing, Randolph was a political tactician who planned nonviolent marches to fight discrimination in the armed forces. Randolph received the Presidential Medal of Freedom and lived to be 90 years old. The National A. Philip Randolph Pullman Porter Museum, founded by Dr. Lyn Hughes in 1995, respects the legacy of Randolph, the Pullman Porters, the BSCP, and other important contributions made by African Americans in the nation's labor movement.

Lexington Betty Smokehouse

756 E. 111th St. • 773-309-8240
www.lexingtonbettysmokehouse.com

✓ While **Pullman National Historical Park** currently doesn't have dining choices available within the park, there is a fun and delicious option located within easy walking distance in the surrounding neighborhood.

Lexington Betty Smokehouse offers Chicago-style barbecue favorites like pulled pork and brisket as well as vegan and vegetarian dishes, complete with soulful sides. What began in 2017 as a food truck endeavor for owner and chef, Dominique Leach, has evolved into a full takeover of the **One Eleven Food Hall** space with a tiered concept that includes not only the restaurant, but also the food truck, catering, and small events. With recent appearances on *Chopped* and Food Network Canada's *Fire Masters*, there has been building excitement around Leach and her grandmother-inspired recipes since the grand opening in August 2022. Part of a massive neighborhood revitalization, which includes the park grounds, Lexington Betty Smokehouse is a must-visit eatery in Pullman.

Lexington Betty Smokehouse (Courtesy of GAZ)

Nearby Alternatives

Discover: Arcade Park

Arcade Park is a green space used by all to enjoy the outdoors. Historically, the formal "carpet bed" gardens featured thousands of annuals sheared in geometric patterns and an area of native wildflowers and plants. Today, the volunteer-led Historic Pullman Garden Club maintains the park with the help of the Chicago Park District.

11132 S. St. Lawrence Ave.
312-747-6576
www.chicagoparkdistrict.com

Discover: Historic Pullman Foundation Pullman Exhibit Hall

Long distance travel was made comfortable with Pullman's sleeping car. In 1877, Pullman went to work on the Pullman Palace Car Works, followed by a plant and town in 1880. Folks are on hand at the exhibit hall to answer questions. Don't miss the mural on the building's north-facing side.

11141 S. Cottage Grove Ave.
773-785-8901
www.pullmanil.org

Discover: Historic Pullman Workers' Homes

A City of Chicago Historic Landmark, National Historic Landmark, and National Monument, the workers' homes from 1880's Pullman Company Town are of great importance. While the protected homes are privately owned, you can still see the diverse architectural elements in houses built for executives, facing the old factory grounds, and tightly knit blockhouses.

103rd St.—115th and S. Cottage Grove Ave.—S. Ellis St.
773-468-9310
www.chicago.gov

Discover: Greenstone Church

Managed by the Greenstone United Methodist Church, Greenstone Church was built in 1882 as an integral part of the original Pullman town. Featuring eye-catching green stone, this 600-seat church has remained mostly unchanged throughout the years, with its original cherrywood altar and pews, pipe organ, and colorful stained-glass windows.

11211 S. St. Lawrence St.
773-928-7870
www.greenstoneunitedmethodistchurchchicago.wordpress.com

Trip Planning

National Park Service

610 E. 111th St.
773-468-9310
www.nps.gov

Courtesy of Wendy Altschuler

Index

Courtesy of Wendy Altschuler